ALFRED'S BASIC ADULT PIANO COURSE

LESSON BOOK · LEVEL TWO

WILLARD A. PALMER · MORTON MANUS · AMANDA VICK LETHCO

With the goal of teaching the adult beginner to play the piano in an enjoyable, quick and easy way, Alfred's Basic Adult Piano Course, Level Two, continues to progress smoothly and easily, without gaps, toward the development of technique and knowledge required to play in all the most frequently used keys. This book begins with an extensive review of the chords and keys previously studied, using fresh and interesting material that will provide enjoyment as well as reinforcement. Particularly significant and noteworthy is the easy presentation of chords in *all positions* in both hands.

The complete reference section that closes the book will enable the student to continue to learn to play scales and chords in all major and minor keys. The pieces used consist of familiar favorites borrowed from folk-song material, themes from operas and the classics, as well as original keyboard compositions.

The student is encouraged to use the compact disc recording or the General MIDI disk. Playing along with these recordings is not only enjoyable, but is invaluable for reinforcing musical concepts such as rhythm, dynamics and phrasing.

CONTENTS

* Track numbers refer to the Compact Disc Recording (#18106).

Review—The Key of C Major

Primary Chords in C Major:

Block chords

Broken chords

DOWN IN THE VALLEY

American Folk Song

Moderato

Down in the val - ley, Val - ley so

low, Late in the eve -

┌EXTENDED POSITION┐

**You are now ready to begin ADULT THEORY BOOK 2
and any of the supplemental volumes listed on page 1.**

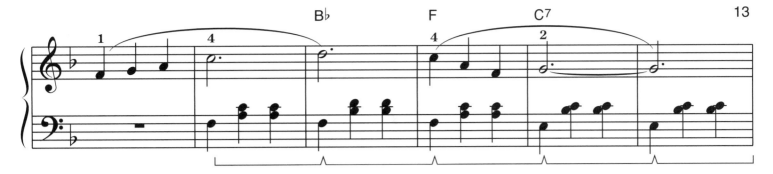

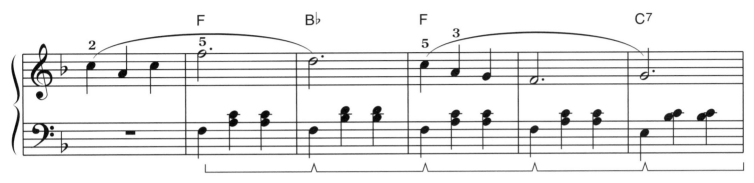

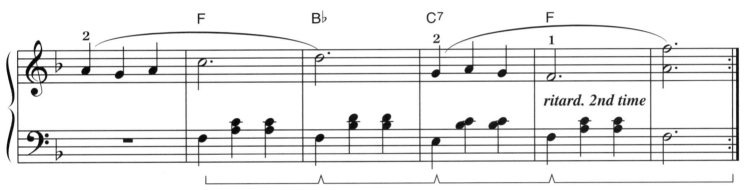

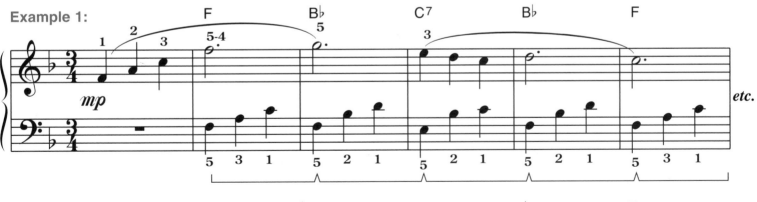

Most popular sheet music has chord symbols above the treble notes just as you can see in *MORNING HAS BROKEN*. You may supply your own LH chords to such music, using BLOCK CHORDS or BROKEN CHORDS in various styles.

OPTIONAL: Play *MORNING HAS BROKEN* again, using broken chords as shown in the following examples. The chords you use should be the same as those indicated by the chord symbols above the treble notes in the music above.

Example 1:

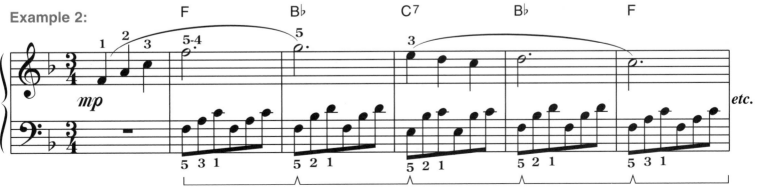

Example 2:

A New Time Signature

6/8 means **6** beats to each measure.
6/8 means an **eighth note** ♪ gets 1 beat.

Clap (or tap) the following rhythms.
Clap **ONCE** for each note, counting aloud.

♪ = EIGHTH note (or ⅞ REST)
Count "1"

Count: 1 2 3 4 5 6 *etc.*

♩ = QUARTER note (or ⁷ REST)
Count "1-2"

Count: 1 2 3 4 5 6 *etc.*

♩• = DOTTED QUARTER note
(or ⁷ ⅞ RESTS)
Count "1-2-3"

Count: 1 2 3 4 5 6 *etc.*

♩• = DOTTED HALF note
Count "1-2-3-4-5-6"
For a WHOLE measure of silence,
a ▬ WHOLE REST is used.

Count: 1 2 3 4 5 6 *etc.*

LA RASPA

A Mexican Stamping Dance

KEY OF F MAJOR
Key Signature: 1 flat (B♭)

Nov. 9/12.

Latin Folk Tune

Allegro
*2nd time accelerando poco a poco al fine**

*Accelerando means *gradually faster.* *Poco a poco* means *little by little.*
Accelerando poco a poco al fine means *gradually faster little by little to the end.*

D. C. al Fine

Beginning

* **sf** = **sforzando,** Italian for "forcing." It means *to play louder on one note or chord;*
in this case it applies to the note above **sf** and the chord below it.

Review—The Key of D Minor

Remember: The keys of F major and D minor are called relatives because they have the same key signature: 1 flat (B♭).

SCHERZO* Nov. 16/12.

KEY OF D MINOR
Key Signature: 1 flat (B♭)

Respectfully dedicated to the memory of world-renowned concert pianist, Vladimir Horowitz.

Andante moderato

Much to my sor-row it's Vlad-i-mir Hor-o-witz Who plays pi-an-o much

bet-ter than I, And pi-an-is-si-mo, al-so for-tis-si-mo,

KEY OF F MAJOR
(relative of D MINOR)

Allegro

I can't be-lieve how his fin-gers can fly! If I just had a mere

por-tion of Vlad-i-mir Hor-o-witz' tal-ent I'd prac-tice all day!

Scherzo. This word means *a musical jest or joke.* It is applied to light and playful pieces.

KEY OF D MINOR

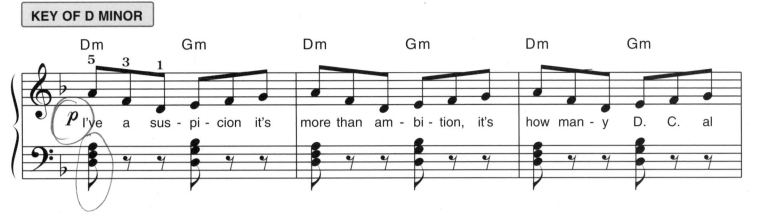

I've a sus - pi - cion it's more than am - bi - tion, it's how man - y D. C. al

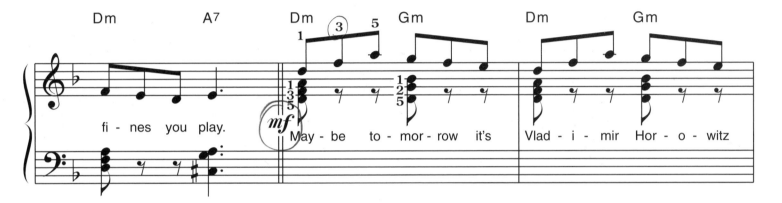

fi - nes you play. May - be to - mor - row it's Vlad - i - mir Hor - o - witz

accelerando poco a poco al fine
Both hands 8va

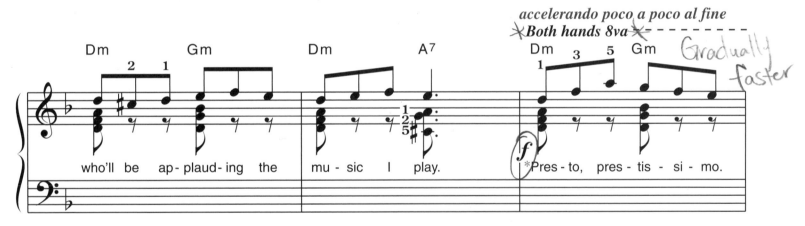

who'll be ap - plaud - ing the mu - sic I play. *Pres - to, pres - tis - si - mo.

Gradually faster

(Both hands 8va)

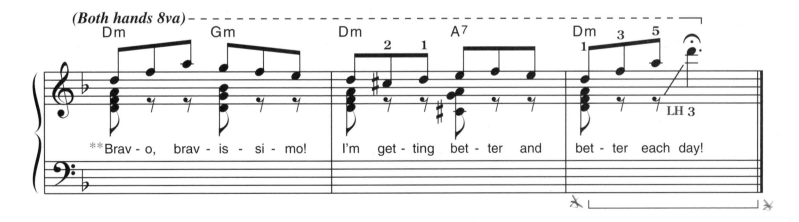

**Brav - o, brav - is - si - mo! I'm get - ting bet - ter and bet - ter each day!

LH 3

*__Presto.__ Italian for "fast." This tempo mark means *faster than* **allegro.**
The word **prestissimo** means *very fast.* It usually means *as fast as possible.*

**__Bravo, bravissimo!__ These Italian words are often shouted by audiences of virtuoso performers.
They can't be exactly translated, but they mean something like *Marvelous,
VERY marvelous!*

Nov. 23 /12.

INTRODUCTION AND DANCE

This very popular folk tune uses mostly the primary chords in D MINOR, but you will also find two D MAJOR TRIADS, plus the **V⁷** and **I** chords in A MINOR and F MAJOR.

The popular song *"Those Were the Days"* was based on this old folk melody.

KEY OF D MINOR
Key Signature: 1 flat (B♭)

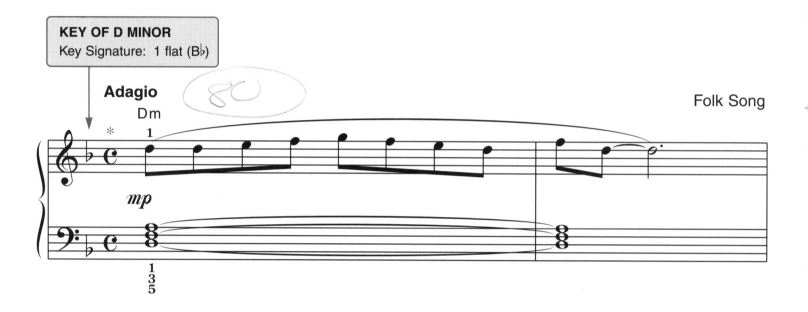

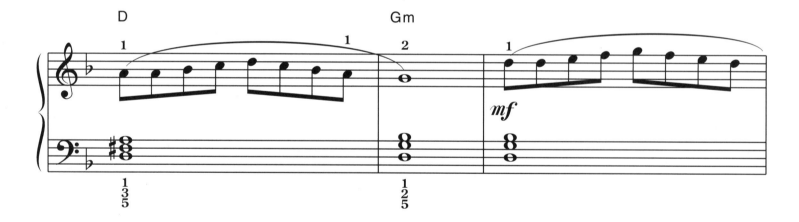

*The time signature **C** indicates COMMON TIME, which is the same as $\frac{4}{4}$ TIME.

120

Allegro

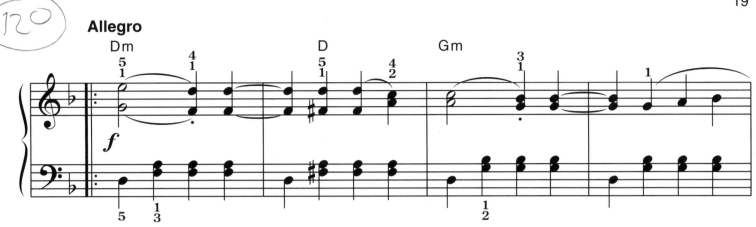

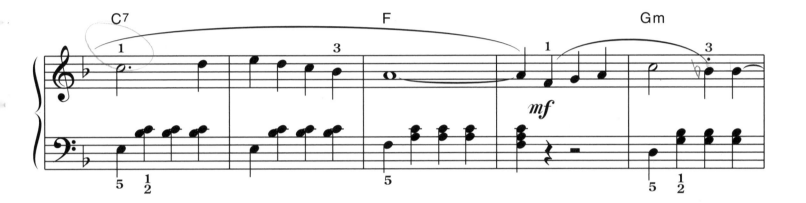

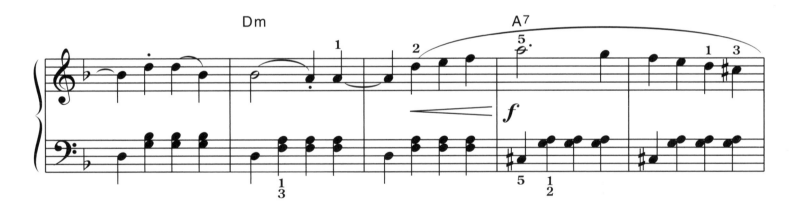

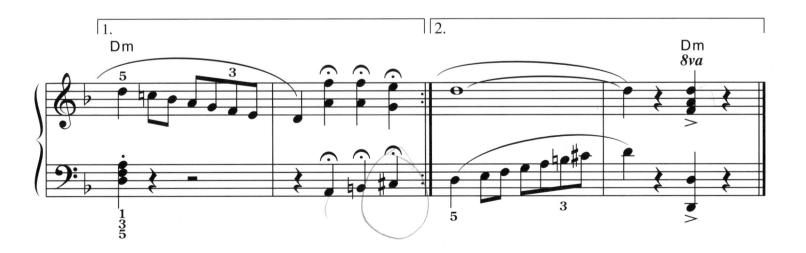

Review—The Key of G Major

Primary chords in G MAJOR:

LA CUCARACHA

Dec. 14/12

KEY OF G MAJOR
Key Signature: 1 sharp (F♯)

Allegro moderato
2nd time 8va

Traditional

*Play the C and D together with the side of the thumb.

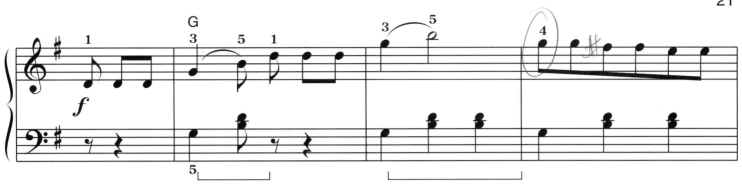

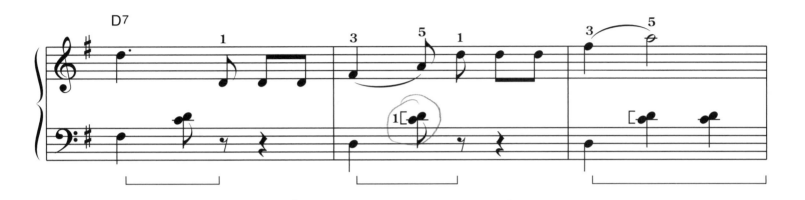

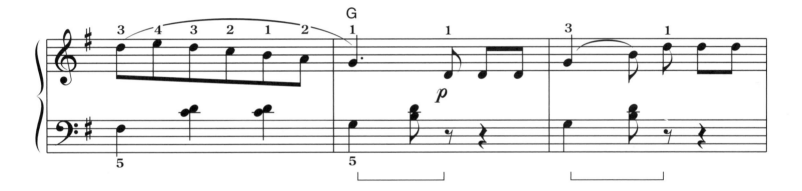

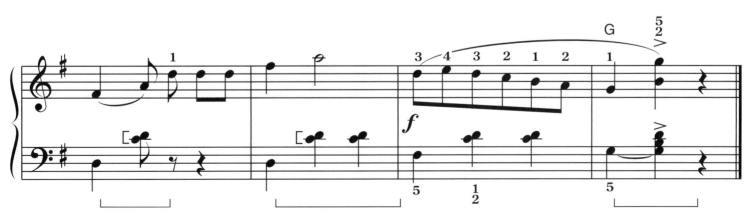

The Key of E Minor (Relative of G Major)

E MINOR is the relative of **G MAJOR.**

Both keys have the same key signature (1 sharp, F#).
REMEMBER: The RELATIVE MINOR begins on the 6th tone of the MAJOR SCALE.

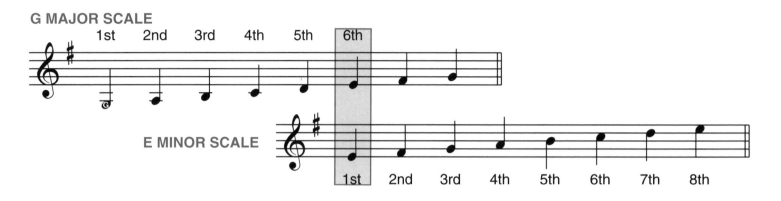

The minor scale shown above is the NATURAL MINOR SCALE.
The natural minor uses only notes that are found in the relative major scale.

The E Harmonic Minor Scale

In the HARMONIC MINOR SCALE, the 7th tone is raised ascending and descending.

The raised 7th in the key of E MINOR is D#. It is not included in the key signature,
but is written as an "accidental" sharp each time it occurs.

Practice the E HARMONIC MINOR SCALE with hands separate. Begin slowly.

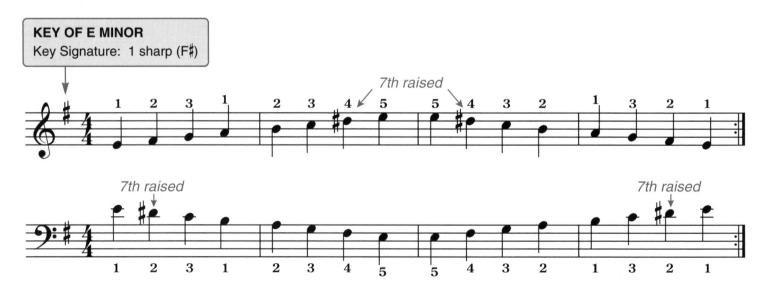

IMPORTANT!   After you have learned the E HARMONIC MINOR SCALE with hands separate, you
may play the hands together in CONTRARY MOTION, by combining the two staffs
above. Notice that both hands play the same numbered fingers at the same time!
Begin with both thumbs on the same E.

THE HOUSE OF THE RISING SUN

KEY OF E MINOR
Key Signature: 1 sharp (F♯)

Folk Song

Andante moderato
2nd time both hands 8va

Ped. simile*

*Ped. simile = Continue to pedal in the same manner.

The Primary Chords in E Minor

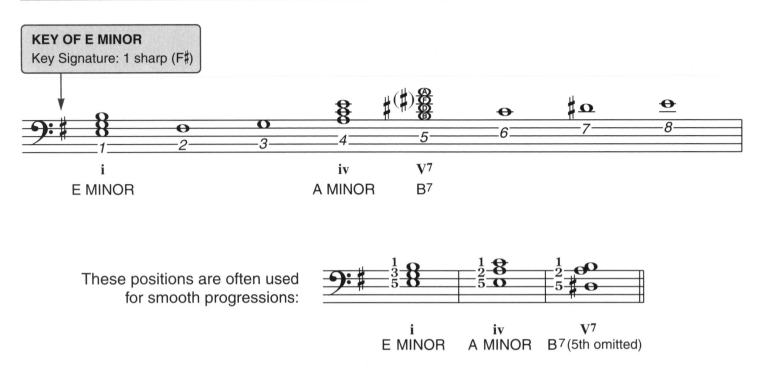

KEY OF E MINOR
Key Signature: 1 sharp (F♯)

i
E MINOR

iv
A MINOR

V⁷
B⁷

These positions are often used
for smooth progressions:

i
E MINOR

iv
A MINOR

V⁷
B⁷ (5th omitted)

E Minor Chord Progression with i, iv, V⁷ chords.

Play several times, saying the chord names and numerals aloud:

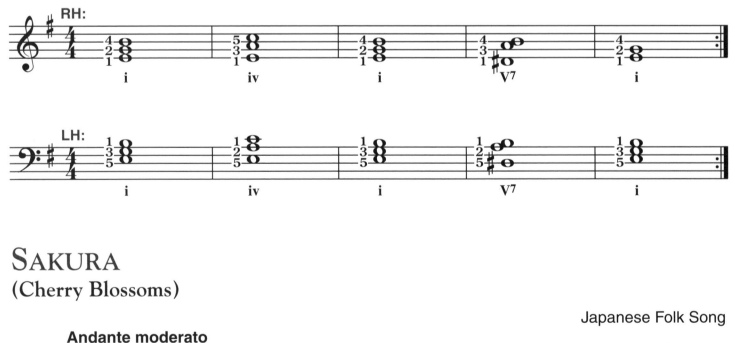

RH:

i   iv   i   V⁷   i

LH:

i   iv   i   V⁷   i

SAKURA
(Cherry Blossoms)

Japanese Folk Song

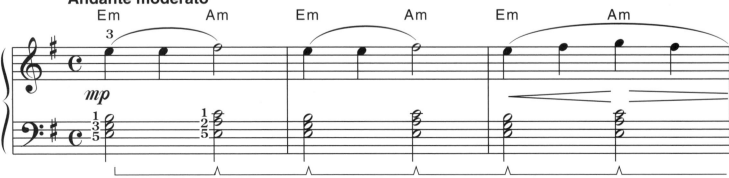

Andante moderato

Em   Am   Em   Am   Em   Am

mp

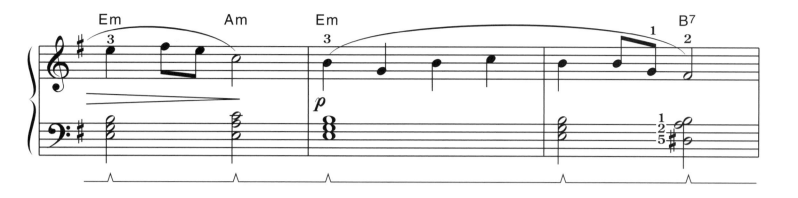

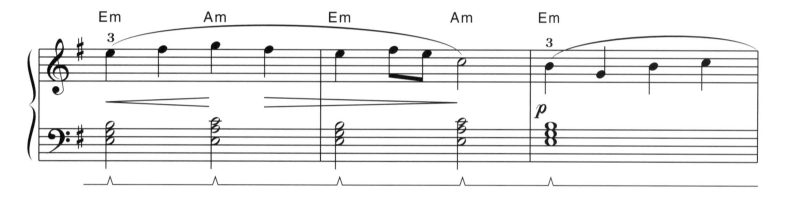

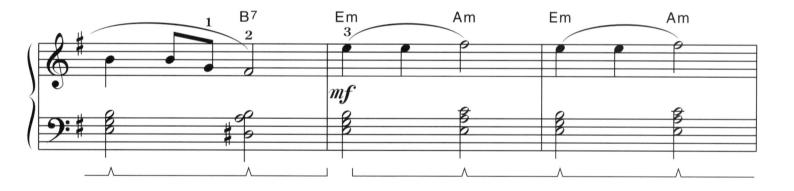

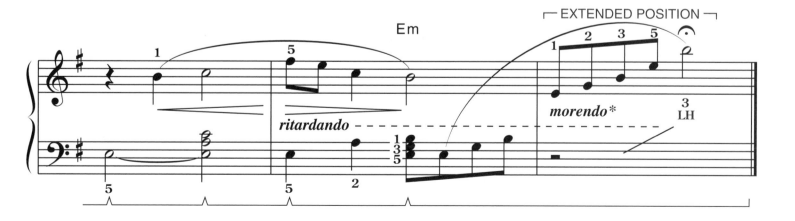

***Morendo** means *dying away.*

E MINOR PROGRESSION with broken **i**, **iv**, & **V⁷** chords. Play several times with LH.

WAVES OF THE DANUBE

KEY OF E MINOR
Key Signature: 1 sharp (F♯)

Melodies from *WAVES OF THE DANUBE* were used
in the popular hit *"THE ANNIVERSARY SONG."*

Moderate waltz tempo

Ivanovici

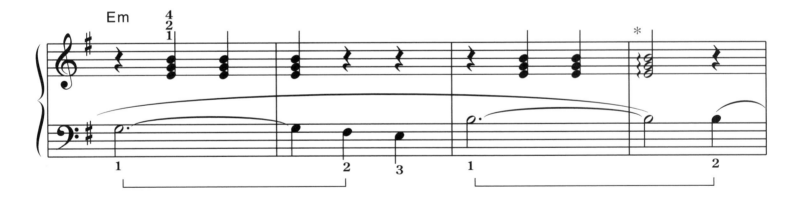

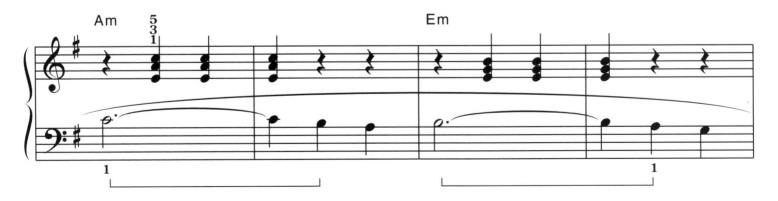

*The wavy line means that the chord is ARPEGGIATED (broken or rolled). Play the lowest note first, and
quickly add the next higher notes one at a time until the chord is complete. The first note is played on the beat.

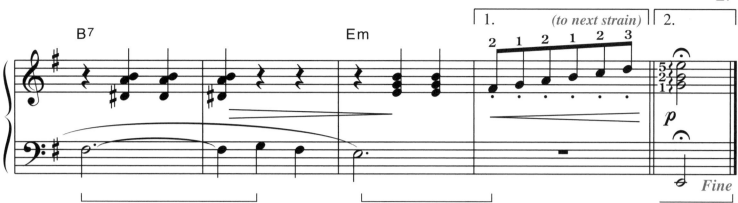

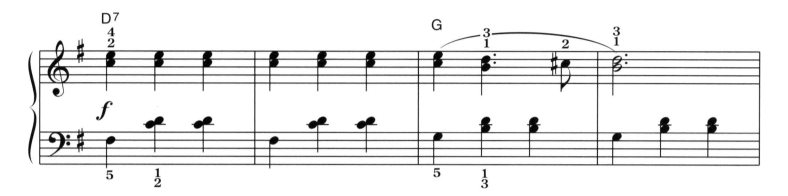

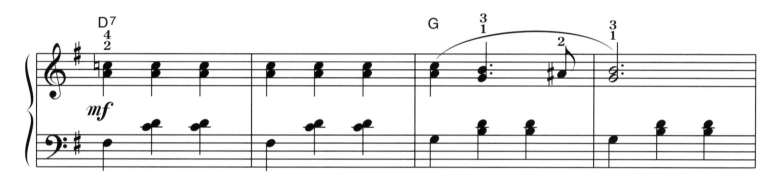

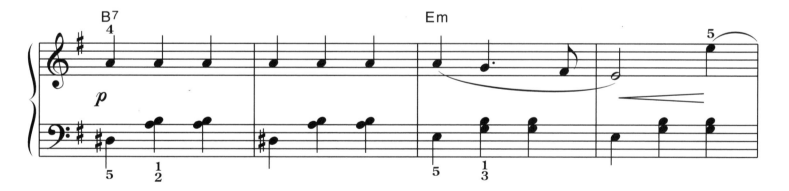

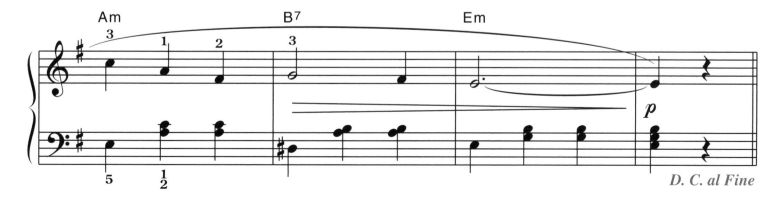

The D Major Scale

Remember that the MAJOR SCALE is made up of two tetrachords *joined* by a whole step.
The second TETRACHORD of the D MAJOR SCALE begins on A.

KEY-NOTE   WHOLE STEP   KEY-NOTE

└─1st TETRACHORD─┘   └─2ND TETRACHORD─┘

> There are 2 sharps (F♯ & C♯) in the D major scale.

The fingering for the D MAJOR SCALE is the same as for the C MAJOR & G MAJOR scales.

Play slowly and carefully!

> **KEY OF D MAJOR**
> Key Signature: 2 sharps (F♯ & C♯)

IMPORTANT! After you have learned the D MAJOR SCALE with hands separate, you may play the hands together in CONTRARY MOTION, as written on the staffs above. Notice that both hands play the same numbered fingers at the same time! Begin with both thumbs on the same D.

ROCK-A MY SOUL

Spiritual

Allegro moderato

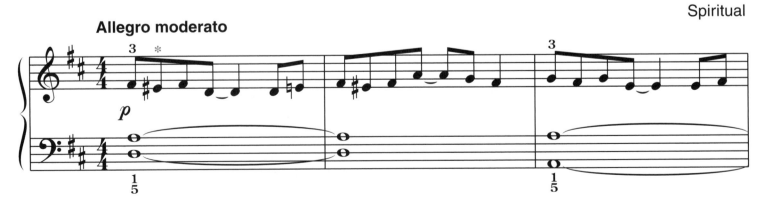

*REMEMBER: Any SHARP sign raises the note one half step. E sharp is the same as F natural!

Pairs of eighth notes may be played a bit unevenly; long-short.

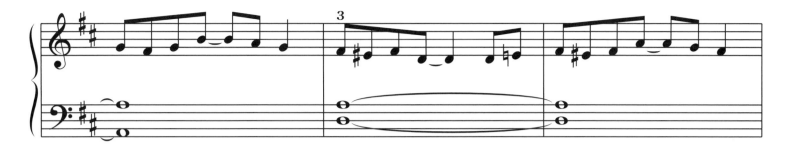

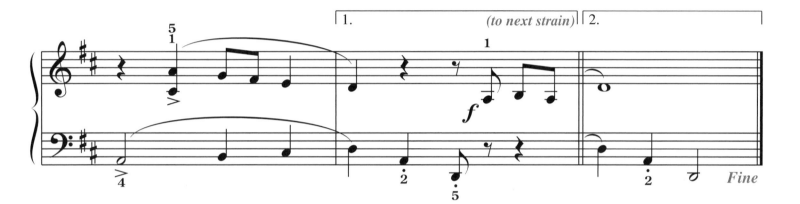

(to next strain)

Fine

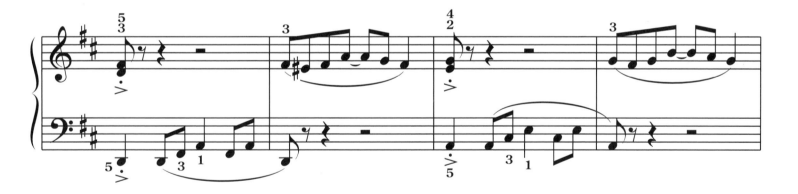

D. C. al Fine

Primary Chords in D Major

Reviewing the D MAJOR SCALE, LH ASCENDING.

KEY OF D MAJOR
Key Signature: 2 sharps (F♯ & C♯)

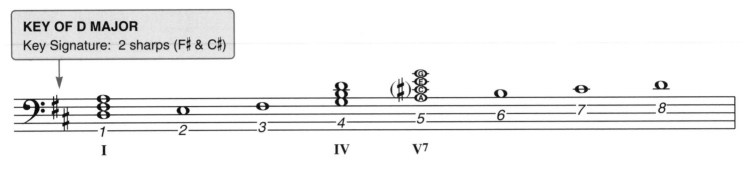

The following positions are often used for smooth progressions:

Primary Chords in D MAJOR

D MAJOR Chord Progression with I, IV, V⁷ chords

Play several times, saying the chord names and numerals aloud:

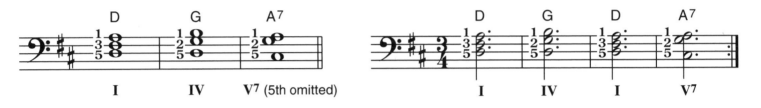

The same, with chords broken two different ways.
Play several times, saying the chord names and numerals aloud.

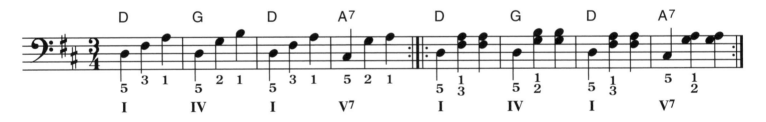

You're in My Heart

(Du, du, liegst mir im Herzen)

Allegro moderato

Folk Song

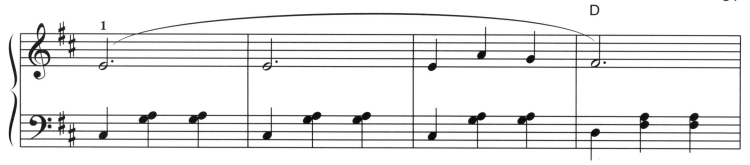

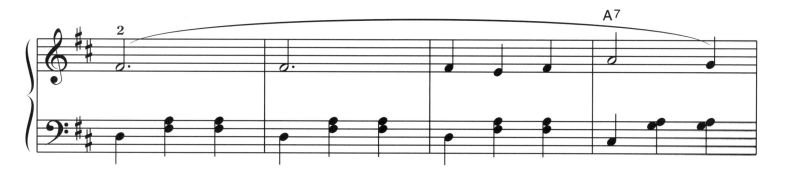

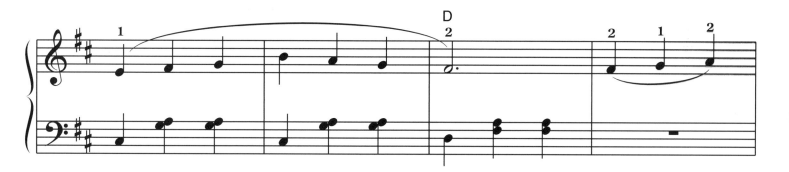

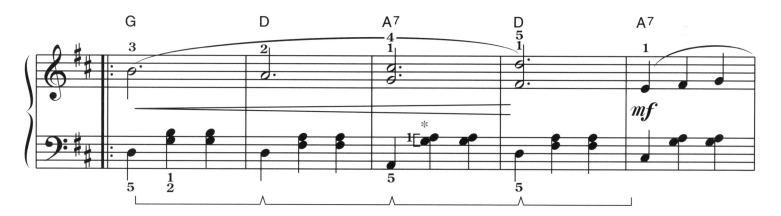

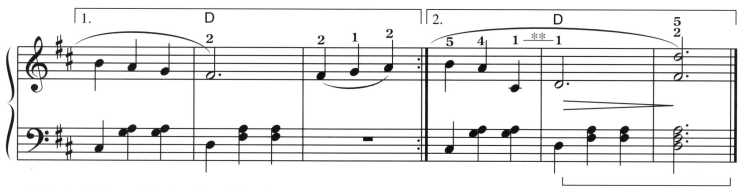

*Play both keys with the side of the thumb.

**Slide the thumb from C♯ to D.

BRAHMS LULLABY

Johannes Brahms

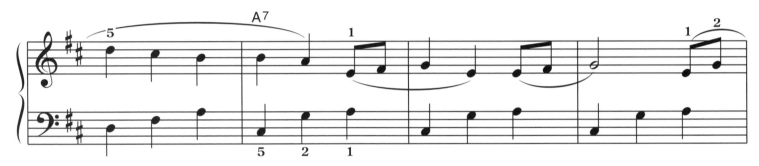

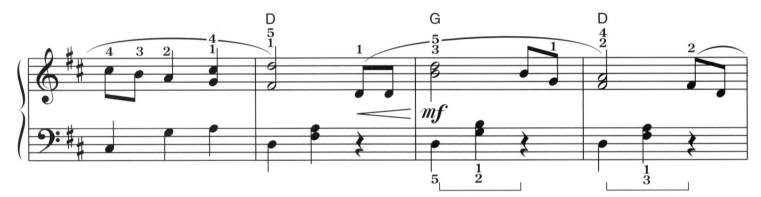

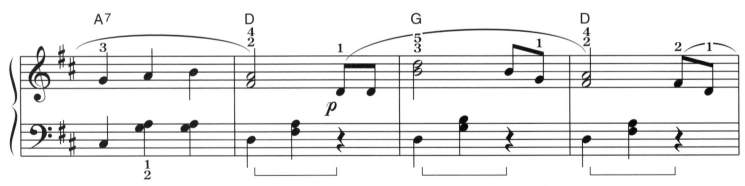

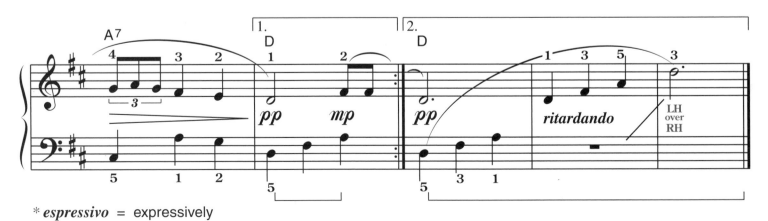

espressivo = expressively

LONESOME ROAD

Folk Song

Andante moderato

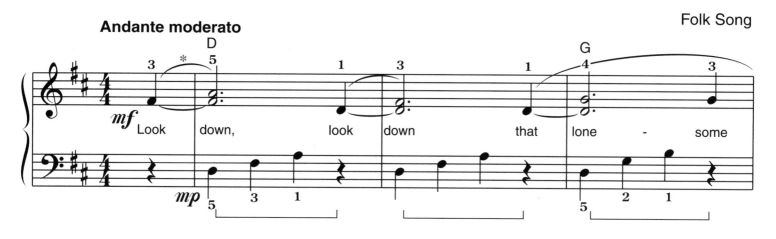

Look down, look down that lone - some

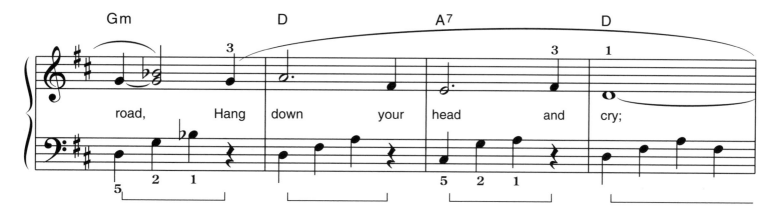

road, Hang down your head and cry;

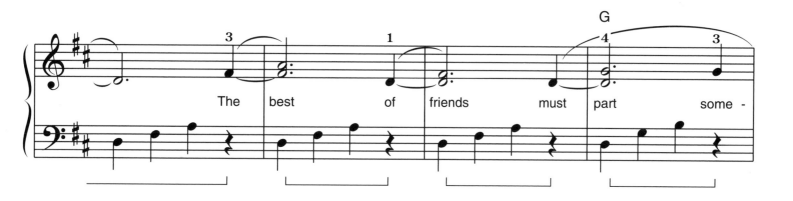

The best of friends must part some -

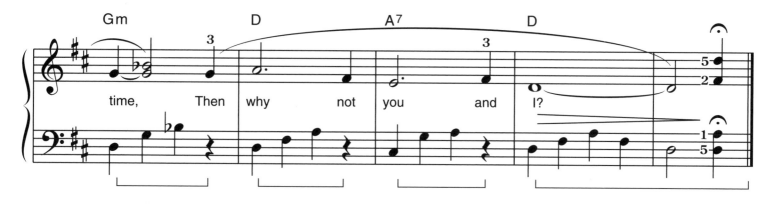

time, Then why not you and I?

*This piece introduces a technic that produces a very legato effect between two melody notes when the second note is part of the same chord. Play the first note and tie it over, holding it as you play the next note.

The Chromatic Scale

The **CHROMATIC SCALE** is made up entirely of **HALF STEPS**.
It goes up and down, using every key, black and white. It may begin on any note.

FINGERING RULES

- Use 3 on each BLACK KEY.
- Use 1 on each white key, except when two white keys are together (no black key between), then use 1-2, or 2-1.

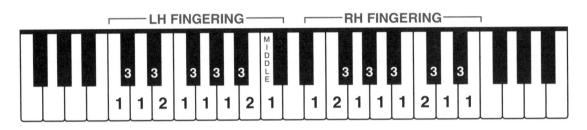

1. Looking at the keyboard above, play the CHROMATIC SCALE with the **LH.** Begin on middle C and GO DOWN one octave.

2. Looking at the keyboard above, play the CHROMATIC SCALE with the **RH.** Begin on E above middle C and GO UP one octave.

Chromatic Warm-Ups

One Octave Chromatic Scale

Play several times daily!

NOTE: It is easy, and fun, to play the CHROMATIC SCALE in CONTRARY MOTION! When the RH begins on E and the LH on C, as above, both hands play the same numbered fingers at the same time.

VILLAGE DANCE

This old folk melody was the inspiration for some of the music of "FIDDLER ON THE ROOF."

Folk Tune

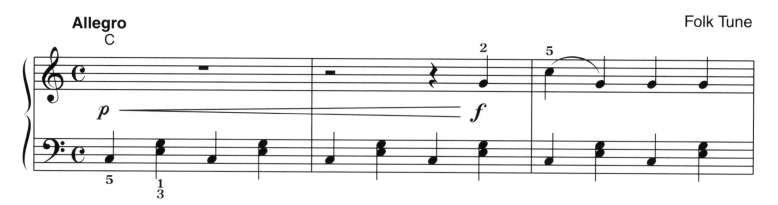

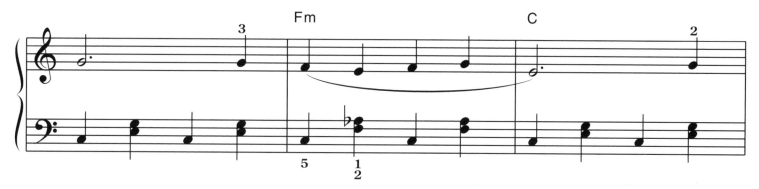

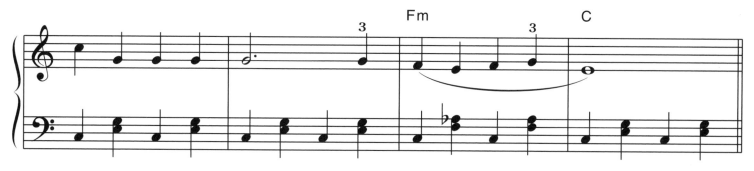

Triads: The 1st Inversion

Any ROOT POSITION TRIAD may be inverted by moving the root to the top.

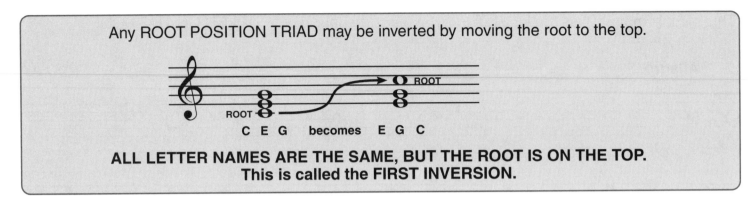

C E G   becomes   E G C

**ALL LETTER NAMES ARE THE SAME, BUT THE ROOT IS ON THE TOP.
This is called the FIRST INVERSION.**

1st INVERSION TRIADS IN C

Play with RH. Use 1 2 5 on each triad. With the fingers properly spaced for the first triad,
you need only move the hand up ONE WHITE KEY for each of the following triads.

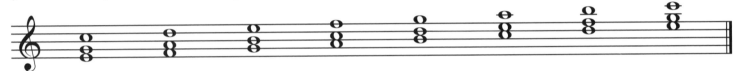

Play the above with LH ONE OCTAVE LOWER. Use 5 3 1 on each triad.

In the 1st inversion, the ROOT
is always the TOP note
of the INTERVAL OF A 4th!

ROOT — This interval is a 4th.
This interval is a 3rd.

In the following line, each triad is played first in its ROOT POSITION, then in the 1st INVERSION.

The important trick in reading these triads easily is this:
   READ ONLY THE LOWEST NOTE of each triad, then add the upper two notes by INTERVAL!

Play with RH.

THE HOKEY-POKEY

All triads down to the first double bar on the next page are 1st inversion triads.
After the double bar, root position triads are also included. READ BY INTERVAL!

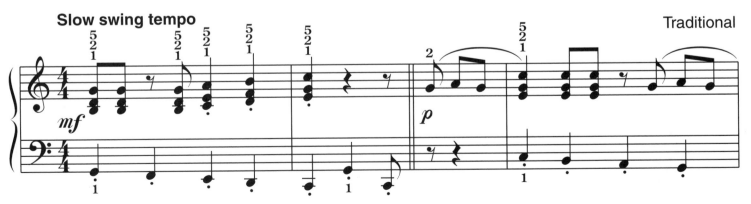

All of the chords in this piece are 1st inversion triads except three.
Find those three and name them before you play.
The eighth notes may be played long-short.

LH staccato

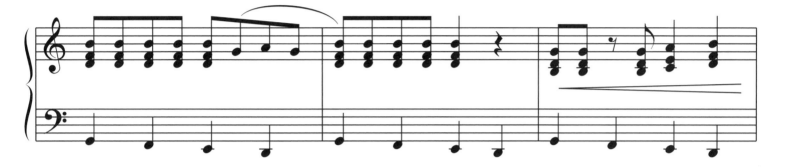

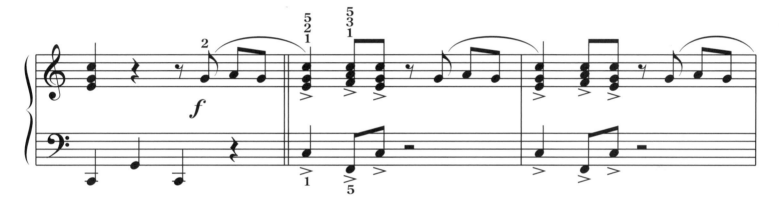

NIGHT SONG

A "Night Song" could also be called a NOCTURNE or a SERENADE.

This piece is much easier than it looks or sounds, because every 3-note chord, including the broken chords in the beginning of the RH, is a 1st inversion triad. They are all fingered 1 2 5 in the RH, or 5 3 1 in the LH.

Andante moderato

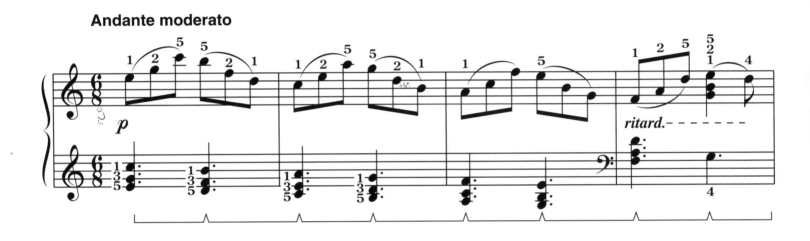

a tempo (resume tempo)

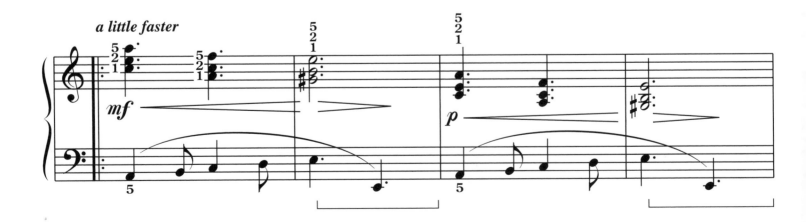

a little faster

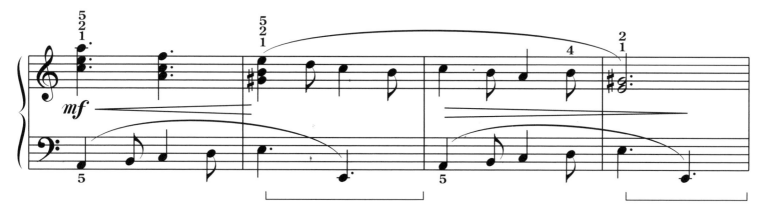

a little slower

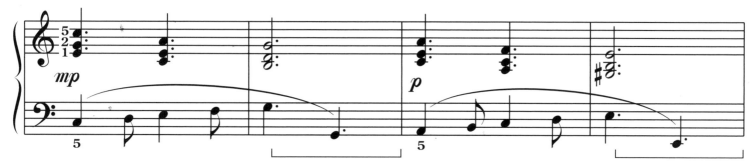

After repeating, D. C. al ⊕, then CODA
(Repeat from the beginning to the sign ⊕,
then skip to the CODA.)

⊕ *CODA (an added ending)*
molto ritardando -

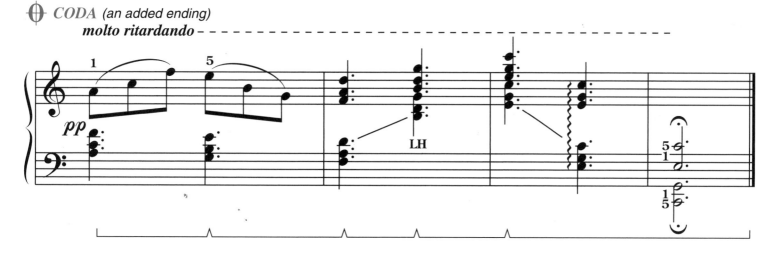

Triads: The 2nd Inversion

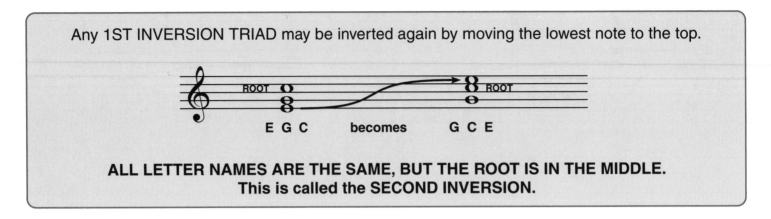

Any 1ST INVERSION TRIAD may be inverted again by moving the lowest note to the top.

ROOT   becomes   ROOT

E G C   becomes   G C E

ALL LETTER NAMES ARE THE SAME, BUT THE ROOT IS IN THE MIDDLE.
This is called the SECOND INVERSION.

2nd INVERSION TRIADS IN C

Play with LH. Use 5 2 1 on each triad. With the fingers properly spaced for the first triad,
you need only move the hand up ONE WHITE KEY for each of the following triads.

Play the above with RH ONE OCTAVE HIGHER. Use 1 3 5 on each triad.

In the 2nd inversion, the ROOT
is always the TOP note
of the INTERVAL OF A 4th!

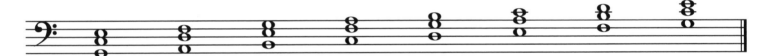

ROOT

This interval is a 3rd.
This interval is a 4th.

In the following line, each ROOT POSITION triad is followed by the same triad in the 1st INVERSION,
then in the 2nd INVERSION. Read only the bottom note of each triad, and add the remaining notes
by INTERVAL!

Play with RH.

REMEMBER: If the root is on the *bottom*, the triad is in **ROOT POSITION**.
If the root is on the *top*, the triad is in the **1st INVERSION**.
If the root is in the *middle*, the triad is in the **2nd INVERSION**.

Play the last line of music above with the RH, saying
"ROOT POSITION, 1st INVERSION, 2nd INVERSION," etc., as you play.

SPACE SHUTTLE BLUES

Play the LH alone first, naming the root of each triad.
Every LH chord is a 2nd inversion triad, so the root is always the MIDDLE note!

Moderate blues tempo

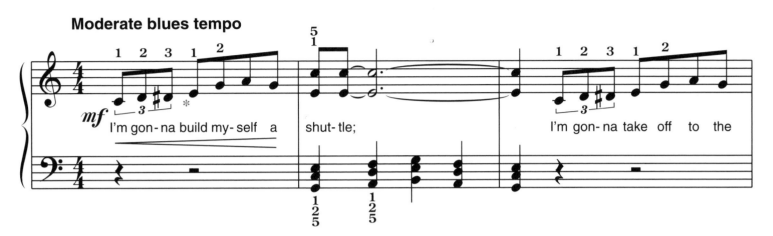

I'm gon-na build my- self a shut- tle; I'm gon-na take off to the

moon! I'm gon-na build my- self a shut- tle;

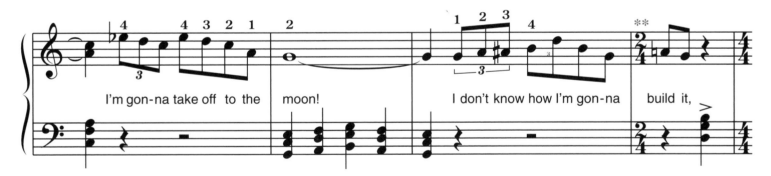

I'm gon-na take off to the moon! I don't know how I'm gon-na build it,

I on- ly know I'll build it soon!

* Play the pairs of eighth notes a bit unevenly, long-short.
** Notice that the time signature changes for one measure only.
In this new time signature: **2** means **2** beats to each measure.
4 means a **quarter note** gets one beat.

Triads in All Positions

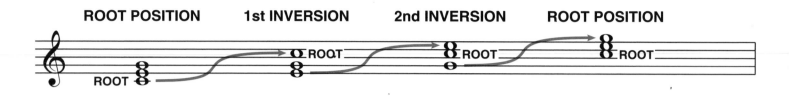

ROOT POSITION   **1st INVERSION**   **2nd INVERSION**   **ROOT POSITION**

Play the following:

C MAJOR TRIAD

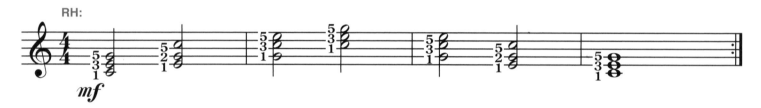

G MAJOR TRIAD

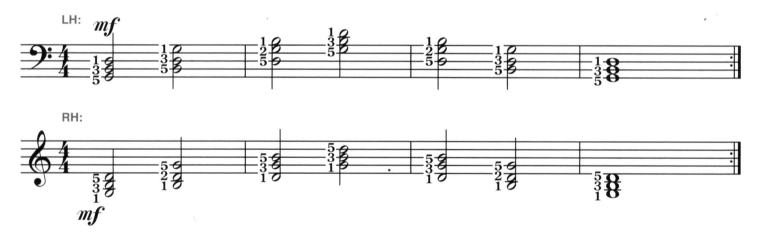

The same, beginning one octave higher:

IMPORTANT!

Repeat all of the above, using ARPEGGIATED CHORDS:  *etc.*

FAREWELL TO THEE (ALOHA OE)

"Aloha Oe" is used in the Hawaiian Islands as a greeting or farewell. This well-known song, which is played and sung for tourists arriving and leaving the islands, was composed by the last queen of the Hawaiian Islands, Lydia Kamekaha Liliuokalani, who reigned in 1891–93.

Adagio

2nd time play both hands 8va throughout

Queen L. K. Liliuokalani

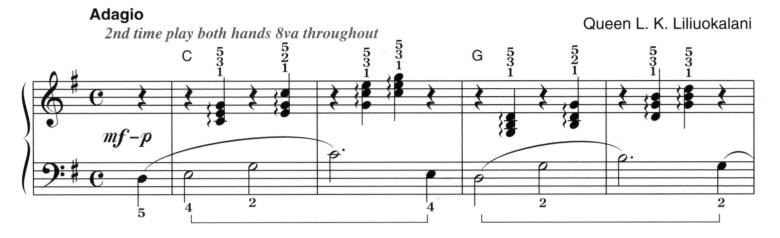

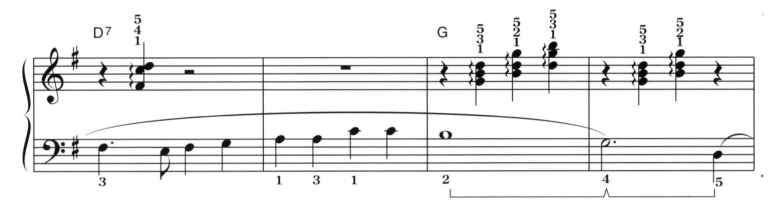

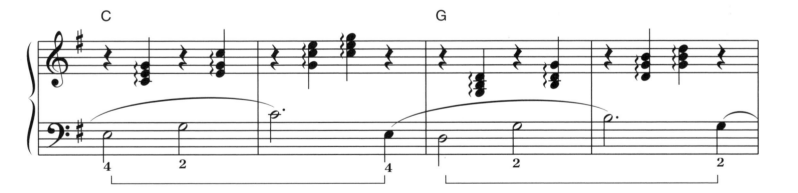

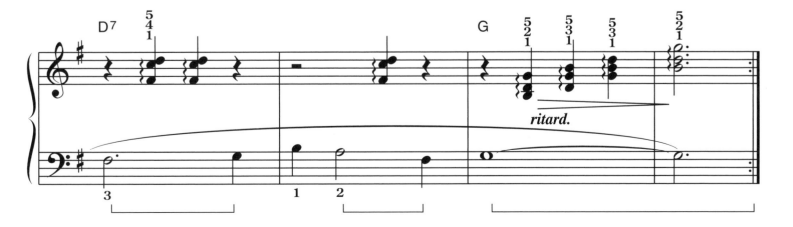

Two-Part Writing

In some music, one hand must play two melodies that have notes of different time values, at the same time.

1st or principal part (the melody). Play with RH.

2nd part (counter-melody). Play with RH.

When both parts are written on ONE staff, the note-stems of the UPPER melody are turned UP, and the note-stems of the LOWER melody are turned DOWN. This is called TWO-PART WRITING.
Play with RH.

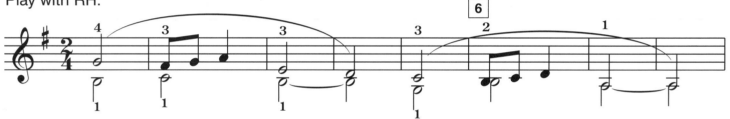

In the 6th measure, the upper (1st) part begins with the eighth note B. The lower (2nd) part has the same B, but it is a half note. Play the B only once, and hold it for the value of the half note while the upper melody continues.

In the 7th and 8th measures, both parts are the same. In this case, the note is given two stems, but it is played only once.

Processional from
POMP AND CIRCUMSTANCE NO. 1

This is one of the most famous of all melodies. It is often played for royal coronation celebrations and for graduation ceremonies.

Sir Edward Elgar

Molto maestoso*

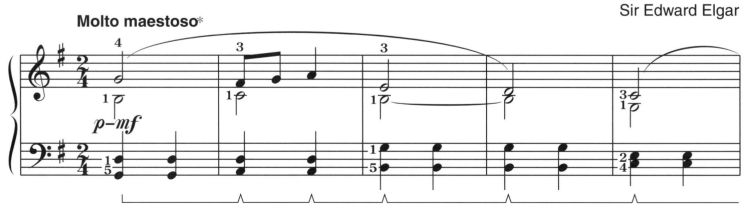

* **Molto** means *very*.   **Molto maestoso** means *very majestically*.

45

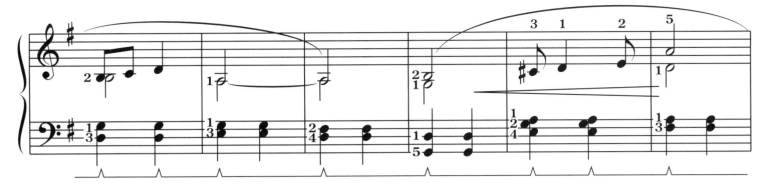

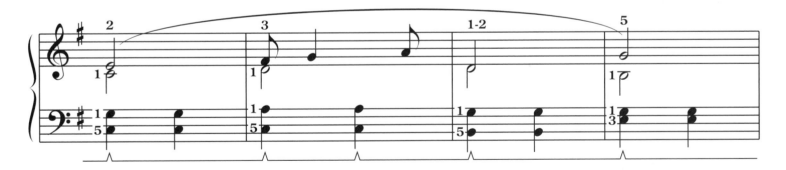

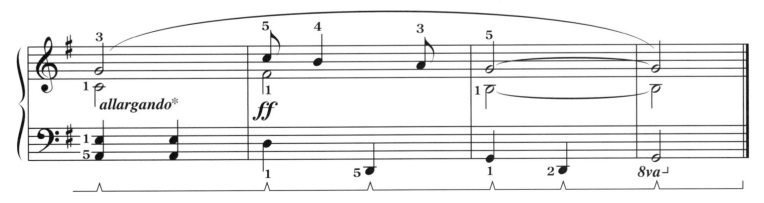

Allargando means *broadening.* It means an increased dignity of style,
slowing the tempo while maintaining or increasing volume.

THE COMPLETE "7th CHORD VOCABULARY"

Play each of the following 7th chords. Stems up = RH. Stems down = LH.

Say the note names as you play.

A C E G

B D F A

C E G B

D F A C

E G B D

F A C E

G B D F

WITH THIS "VOCABULARY" YOU CAN PLAY 7th CHORDS IN ANY KEY, SIMPLY BY USING THE KEY SIGNATURE.

MEMORIZE THE COMPLETE "7th CHORD VOCABULARY."

Seventh Chord Review

A **SEVENTH CHORD** may be formed by adding to the ROOT POSITION TRIAD a note that is a SEVENTH above the root.

The four notes of a seventh chord are:

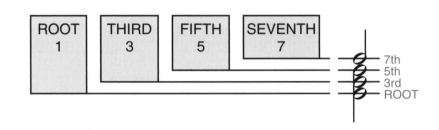

SEVENTH CHORDS in **ROOT POSITION** (with root at the bottom) look like this:

The 5th is often omitted from the seventh chord. This makes it simple to play with one hand.

Play with LH.

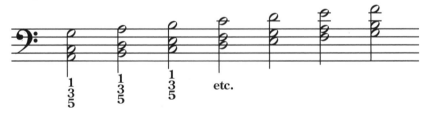

The 3rd is sometimes omitted.

Play with LH.

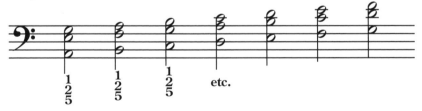

All seventh chords on this page are in **ROOT POSITION!**

REMEMBER: When the interval from the lowest note of the chord to the highest is a 7th, the BOTTOM NOTE is the ROOT!

SWINGING SEVENTHS

Every LH chord in this piece is a seventh chord in root position! Play the LH alone at first.
Notice which seventh chords have the 5th omitted and which have the 3rd omitted.

Moderately slow, with a "swing feeling"

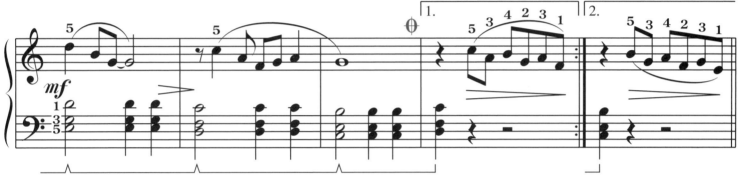

D. C. al ⊕, then CODA

⊕ *CODA*

Inversions of Seventh Chords

Four-note seventh chords may be played in the following positions.
All note-names are the same in each position, but in a different order!

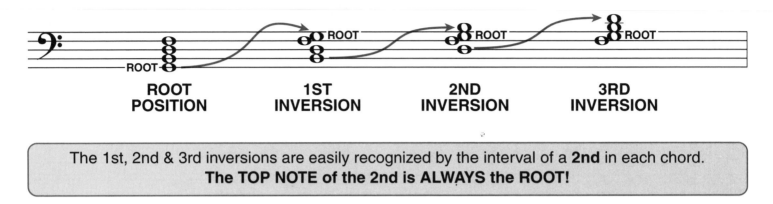

ROOT POSITION   **1ST INVERSION**   **2ND INVERSION**   **3RD INVERSION**

The 1st, 2nd & 3rd inversions are easily recognized by the interval of a **2nd** in each chord.
The TOP NOTE of the 2nd is ALWAYS the ROOT!

Here are some 7th chords with omitted 5ths or 3rds. Play the LH as written,
then the RH one octave higher.

1. The G^7 chord is the V^7 chord in the key of C MAJOR. Its notes are **G B D F.**

   5th (D) omitted: 3rd (B) omitted:

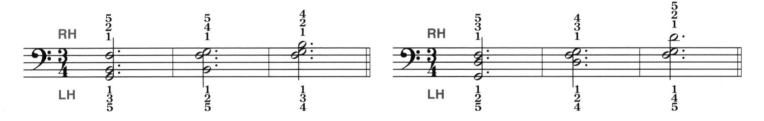

2. The D^7 chord is the V^7 chord in the key of G MAJOR. Its notes are **D F♯ A C.**

   5th (A) omitted: 3rd (F♯) omitted:

3. The C^7 chord is the V^7 chord in the key of F MAJOR. Its notes are **C E G B♭.**

   5th (G) omitted: 3rd (E) omitted:

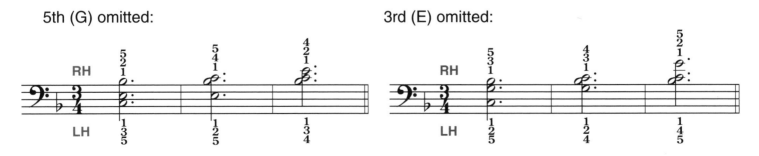

AMERICA, THE BEAUTIFUL

Samuel A. Ward

Andante

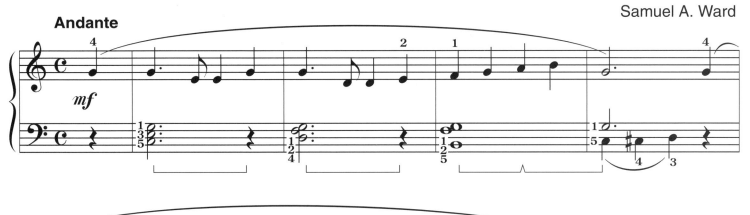

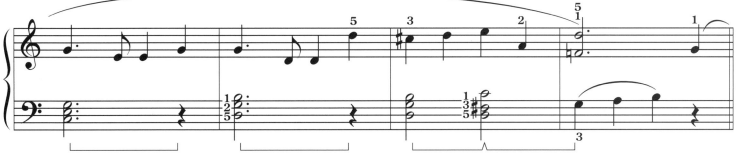

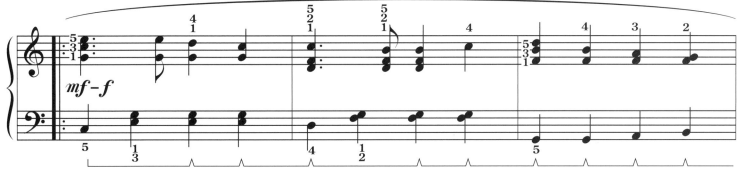

2nd time molto maestoso

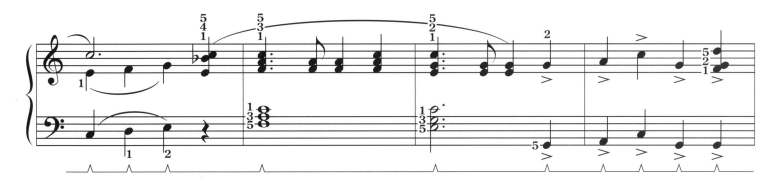

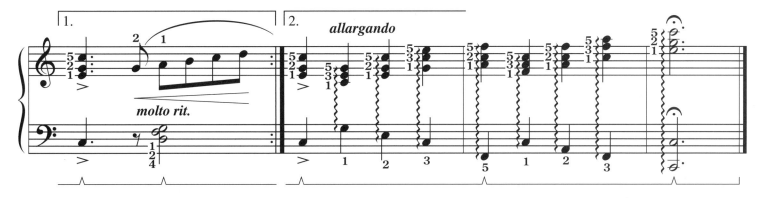

Draw an arrow to the root of each 7th chord.

Theme from
THE POLOVETSIAN DANCES

This melody from Borodin's opera "Prince Igor" was used in the 1953 Broadway musical "Kismet," as the basis for the very popular song, "Stranger in Paradise."

See if you can identify all the seventh chords.

A. Borodin

Eighth notes should be played evenly!

*OPTIONAL: Roll each LH chord. Pedal as you wish.

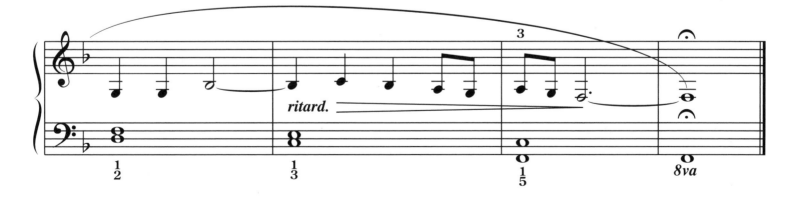

Sixteenth Notes

When one sixteenth note is written alone, it looks like this:

Sixteenth notes are usually in **pairs** or **groups of four,** written like this:

OR

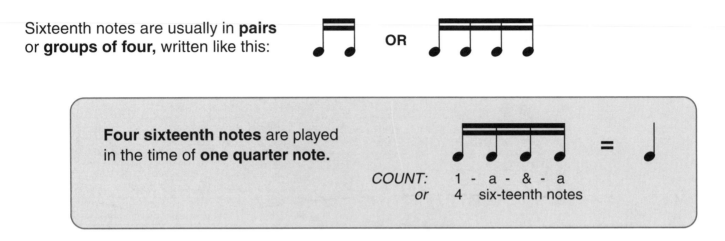

> **Four sixteenth notes** are played in the time of **one quarter note.**
>
> *COUNT:* 1 - a - & - a
> *or* 4 six-teenth notes

There can be 16 sixteenth notes in one measure of **COMMON (4/4) TIME!**

Play several times: first ADAGIO, then ANDANTE, then ALLEGRO MODERATO.

> **Two sixteenth notes** are played in the time of **one eighth note.**

Play several times: first ADAGIO, then ANDANTE, then ALLEGRO MODERATO.

ARKANSAS TRAVELER

Allegro moderato

American Folk Tune

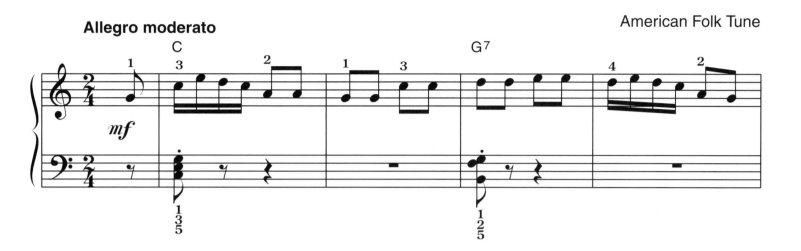

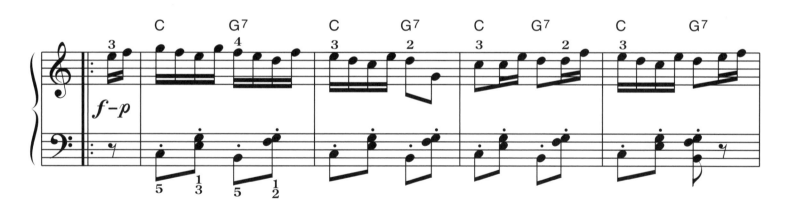

D. C. al Fine

Anna Magdalena Bach's notebook may be the most famous musical collection in the world. It was probably presented by Johann Sebastian Bach, one of the greatest musicians of all time, to his wife, Anna Magdalena, as a birthday present. It must have been a delight to the eye when it was new. The initials "A. M. B." and the date "1725" were stamped on the cover in gold. The book was green with gold borders, two locks and a red satin ribbon. In this book the members of the Bach family were to write many of their favorite pieces. No one knows who actually composed this famous MUSETTE. It is in the handwriting of Anna Magdalena. In the original manuscript there are no indications of tempo, dynamics, fingering, phrasing, staccato, etc. These have all been added by the editor. This MUSETTE has been recorded by many celebrated keyboard artists.

MUSETTE

From *ANNA MAGDALENA BACH'S NOTEBOOK*

Moderato

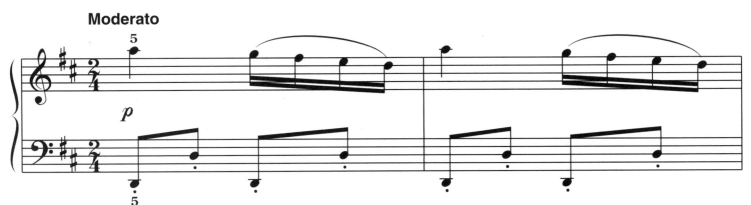

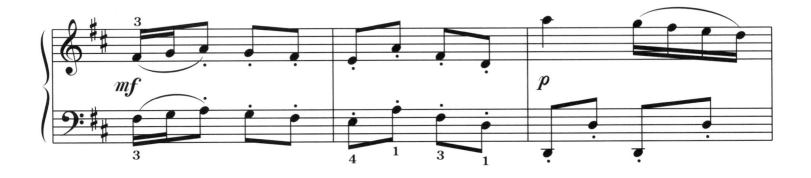

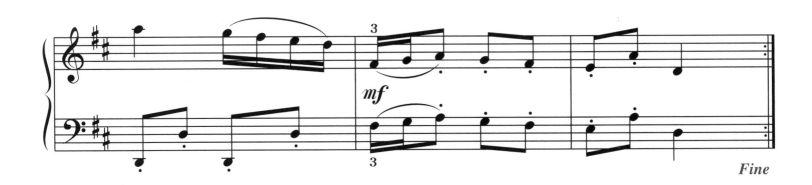

Fine

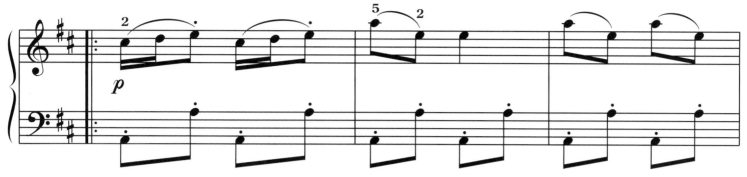

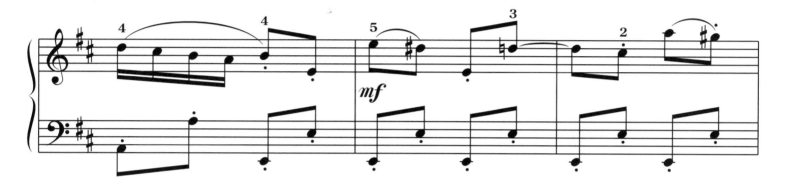

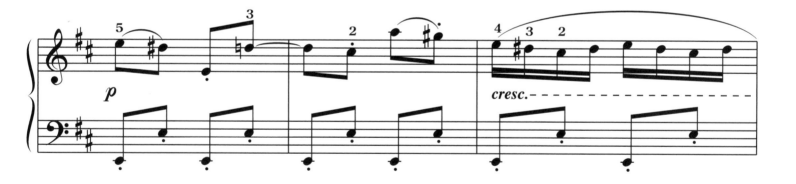

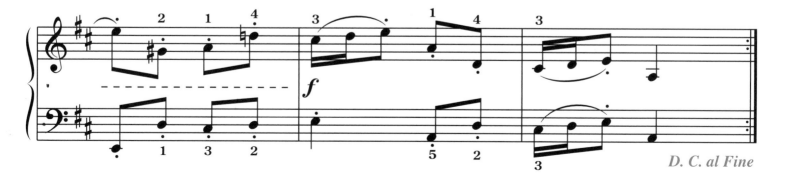

D. C. al Fine

Theme from MUSETTA'S WALTZ

(from "La Bohème")

Giacomo Puccini

Moderately slow

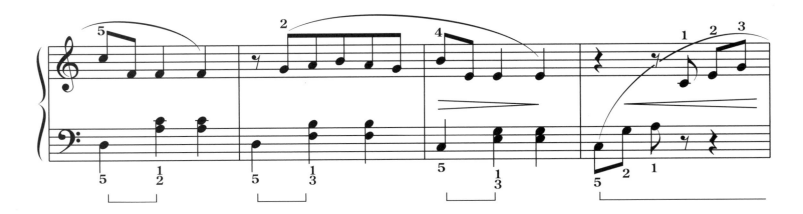

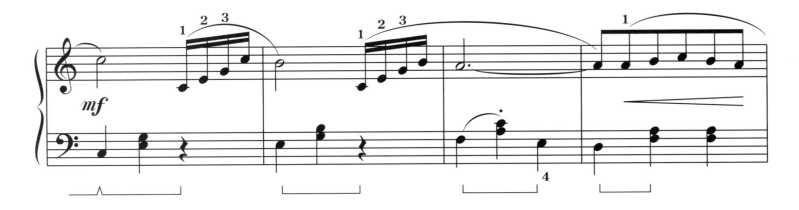

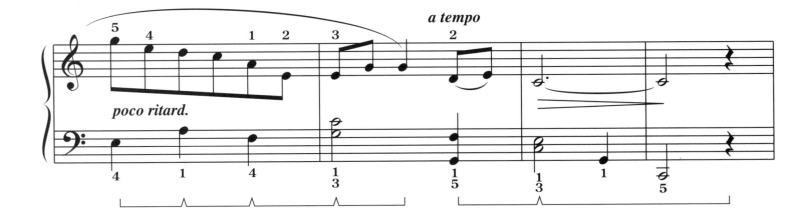

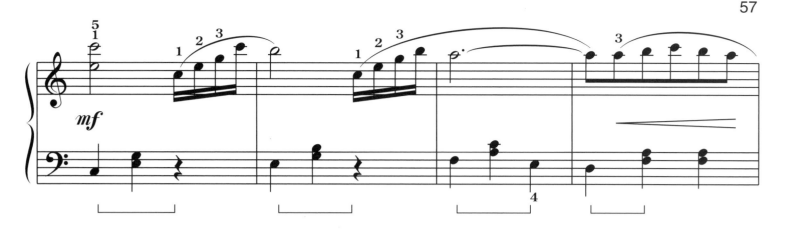

The Dotted Eighth Note

A DOTTED EIGHTH NOTE has the same value as an eighth note tied to a sixteenth note.

Count aloud and play:

COUNT: 1 a & a etc.

The following line should sound exactly the same as the above line.
The only difference is the way it is written.

COUNT: 1 a & a etc.

THE BATTLE HYMN OF THE REPUBLIC

Steffe-Howe

Slow march tempo

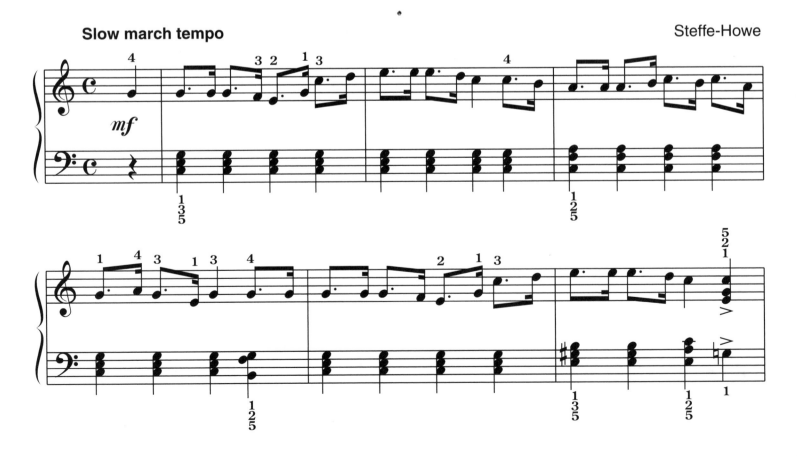

Maestoso

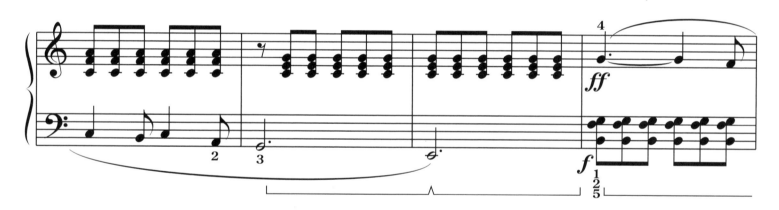

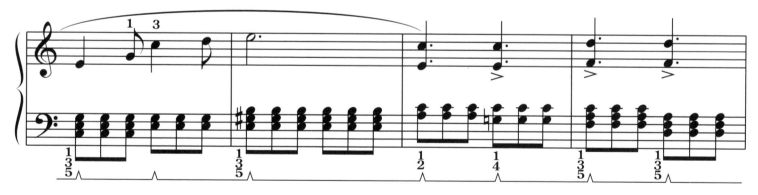

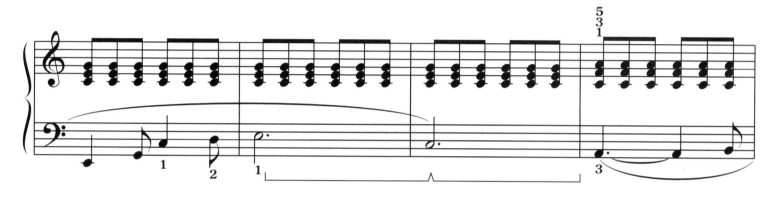

The B♭ Major Scale

REMEMBER! The MAJOR SCALE is made of TWO TETRACHORDS joined by a WHOLE STEP.
The pattern of each tetrachord is: WHOLE STEP—WHOLE STEP—HALF STEP.

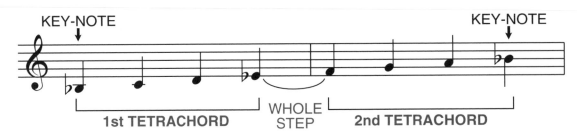

The fingering for the B♭ MAJOR SCALE is irregular. The 5th finger is not used in either hand.
The RH plays the key note, B♭, with the 4th finger. The fingering groups then fall
1 2 3 - 1 2 3 4 ascending, then 4 3 2 1 - 3 2 1 descending, ending on 4.

Play slowly and carefully!

KEY OF B♭ MAJOR
Key Signature: 2 flats (B♭ & E♭)

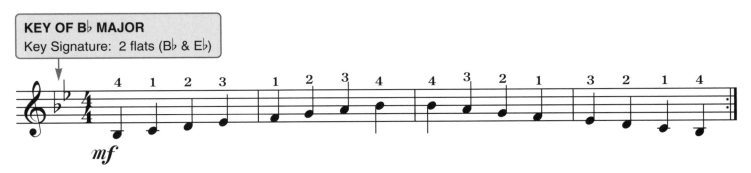

The LH plays the key note, B♭, with the 3rd finger. The fingering groups then fall
1 2 3 4 - 1 2 3 descending, then 3 2 1 - 4 3 2 1 ascending, ending on 3.

Play slowly and carefully!

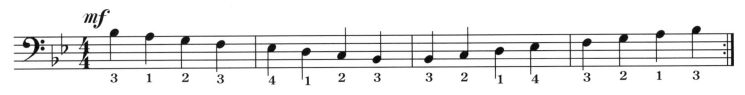

THE RIDDLE

The popular song "The Twelfth of Never" was based on this well-known folk melody.

Folk Song

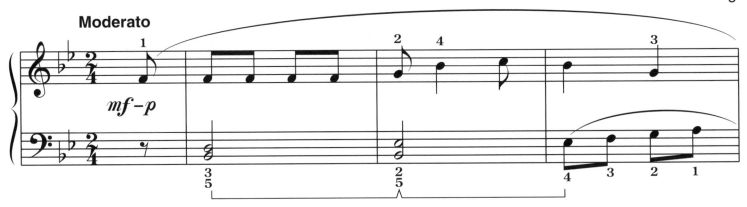

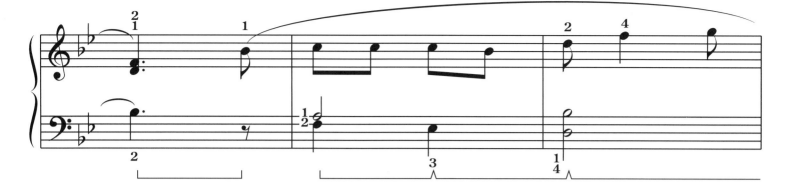

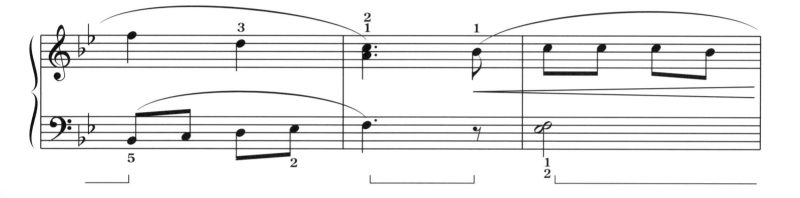

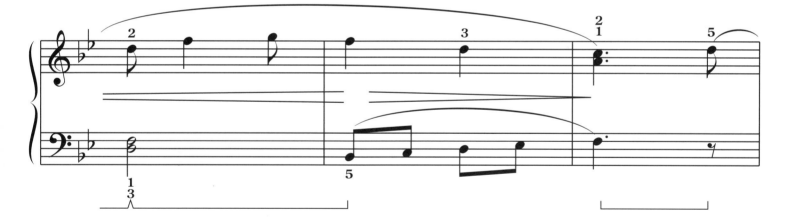

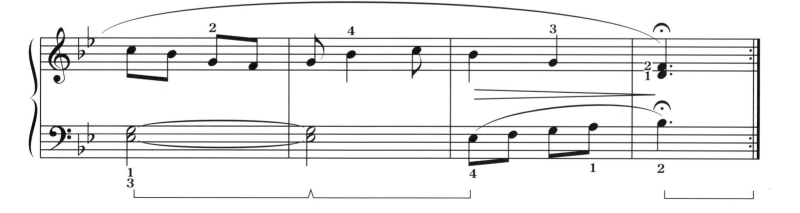

The Primary Chords in B♭ Major

Reviewing the B♭ MAJOR SCALE, LH ascending.

KEY OF B♭ MAJOR
Key Signature: 2 flats (B♭ & E♭)

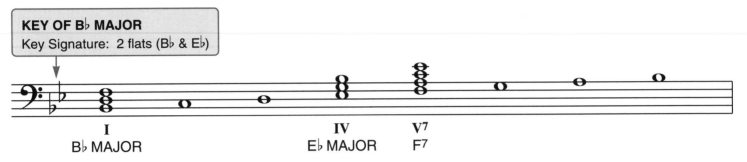

I   IV   V7
B♭ MAJOR   E♭ MAJOR   F7

The following positions are often used for smooth progressions:

I   IV   V7
B♭ MAJOR   E♭ MAJOR   F7 (5th omitted)

B♭ Major Chord Progression with I, IV & V7 chords

Play several times, saying the chord names and numerals aloud:

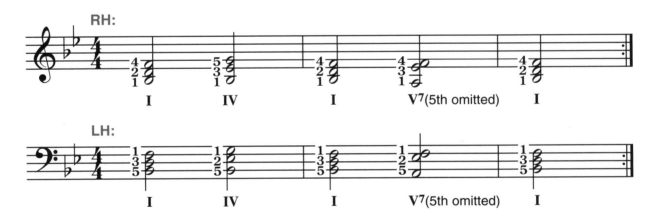

RH:
I   IV   I   V7(5th omitted)   I

LH:
I   IV   I   V7(5th omitted)   I

NOBODY KNOWS THE TROUBLE I'VE SEEN

Spiritual

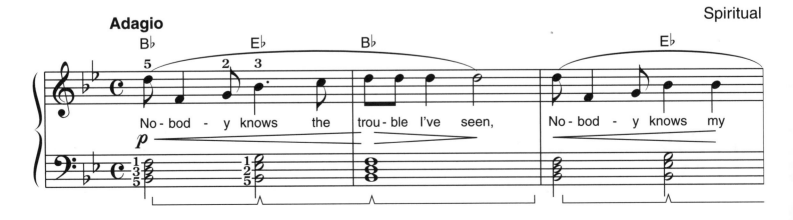

No-bod-y knows the trou-ble I've seen, No-bod-y knows my

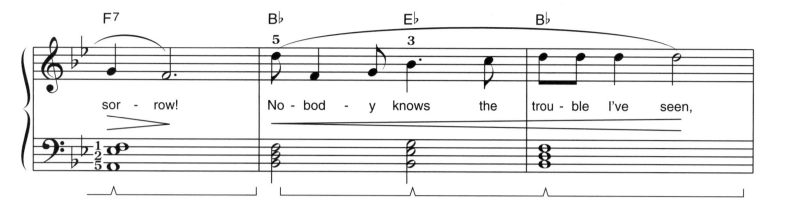

sor - row! No - bod - y knows the trou - ble I've seen,

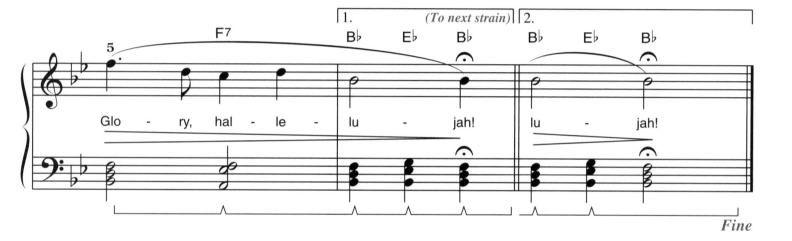

Glo - ry, hal - le - lu - jah! lu - jah!

Fine

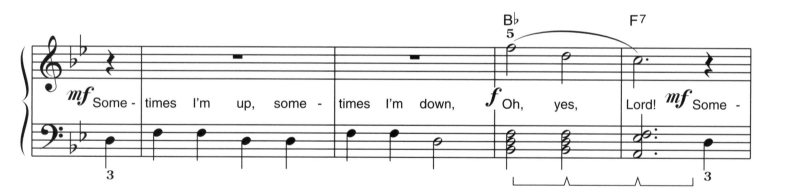

Some - times I'm up, some - times I'm down, Oh, yes, Lord! Some -

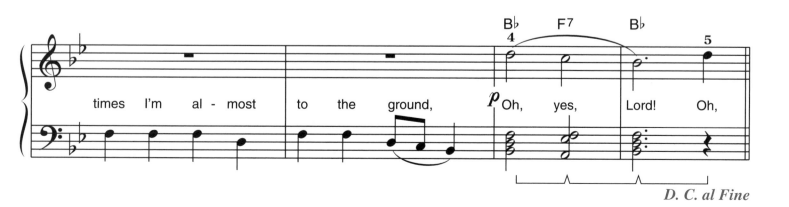

times I'm al - most to the ground, Oh, yes, Lord! Oh,

D. C. al Fine

LA DONNA E MOBILE

(from "Rigoletto")

This is one of the most popular operatic songs ever written. The rest in the 8th measure of
the introduction must have come as quite a surprise at the first performance, and it still lends
the piece a certain special charm. The entire piece may be played twice, right from the
beginning, including the repeated two lines, since that is the way it is performed in the opera.

Giuseppe Verdi

Allegro moderato

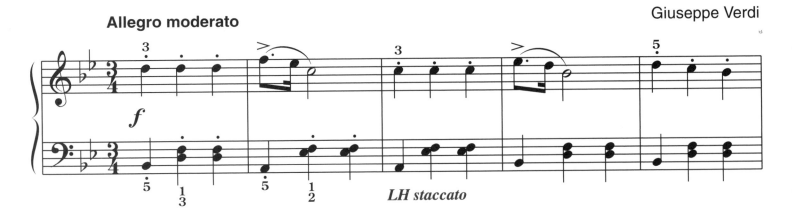

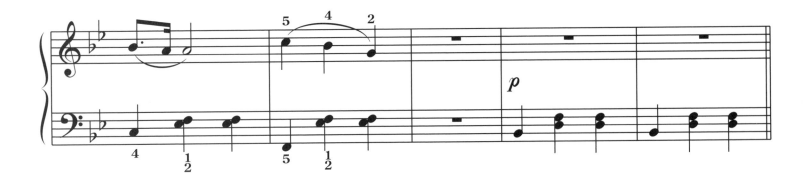

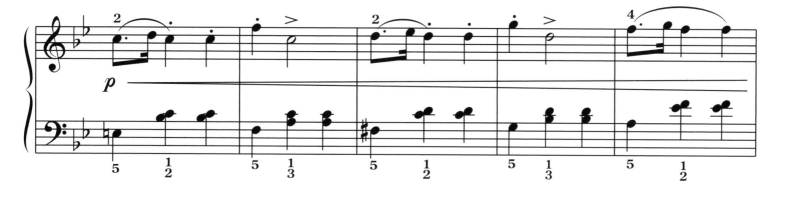

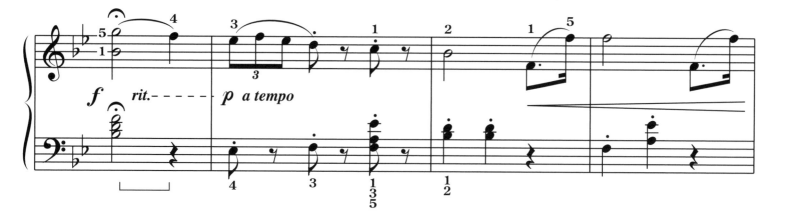

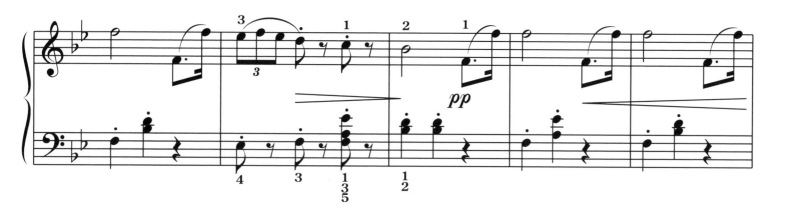

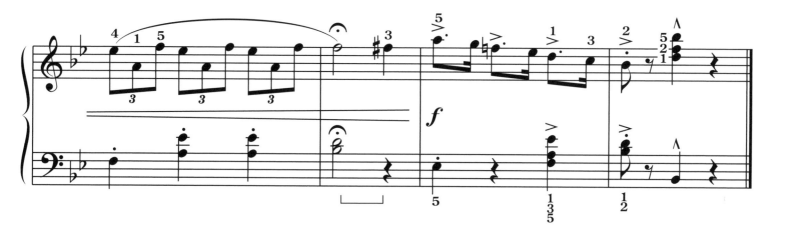

FRANKIE AND JOHNNIE

This "eight-to-the-bar" style is known as "Boogie Woogie."
Play with a driving rhythm, with the eighth notes in long-short pairs.
This is an excellent review in syncopation, and is fun to play.

Traditional

Play both black keys with the side of the thumb!

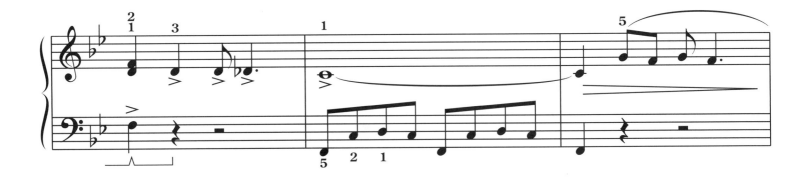

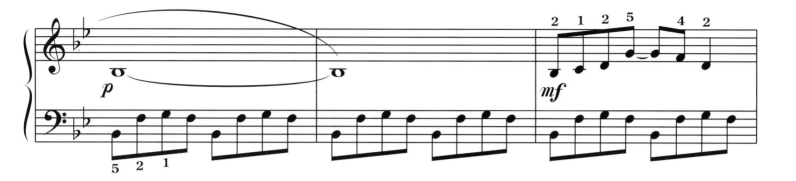

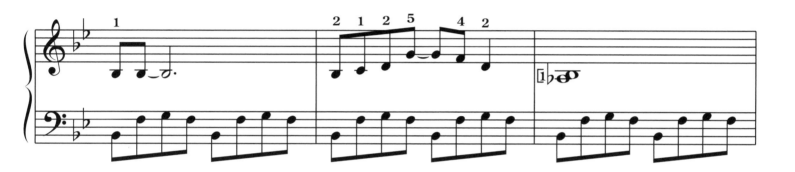

The Key of G Minor (Relative of B♭ Major)

G MINOR is the relative of **B♭ MAJOR.**
Both keys have the same key signature (2 flats, B♭ & E♭).
REMEMBER: The RELATIVE MINOR begins on the 6th tone of the MAJOR SCALE.

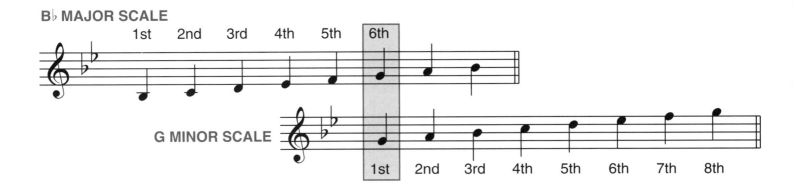

The minor scale shown above is called the NATURAL MINOR SCALE.
It uses only notes that are found in the relative major scale.

The G Harmonic Minor Scale

In the HARMONIC MINOR SCALE, the 7th tone is raised ascending and descending.
The raised 7th in the key of G MINOR is F♯. It is not included in the key signature,
but it is written as an "accidental" sharp each time it occurs.

Practice the G HARMONIC MINOR SCALE with hands separate. Begin slowly.

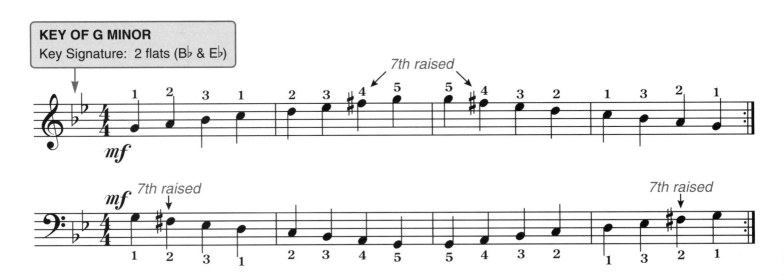

IMPORTANT! After you have learned the G HARMONIC MINOR SCALE with hands separate, you may
play the hands together in CONTRARY MOTION, by combining the two staffs above.

BLACK IS THE COLOR OF MY TRUE LOVE'S HAIR

KEY OF G MINOR
Key Signature: 2 flats (B♭ & E♭)

Folk Song

* // = *Caesura* (pronounced *say-ZHUR-ah,* but usually called "railroad tracks").
   This indicates a momentary interruption of the melody with silence.

The Primary Chords in G Minor

Reviewing the G MINOR SCALE, LH ascending.

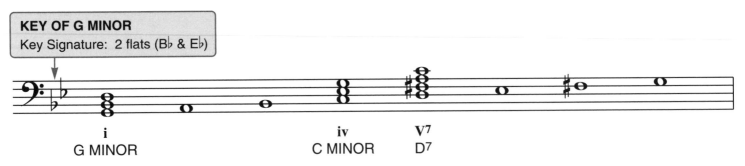

The following positions are often used for smooth progressions:

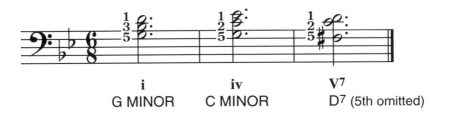

G MINOR PROGRESSION with i, iv & V⁷ chords. Play several times.

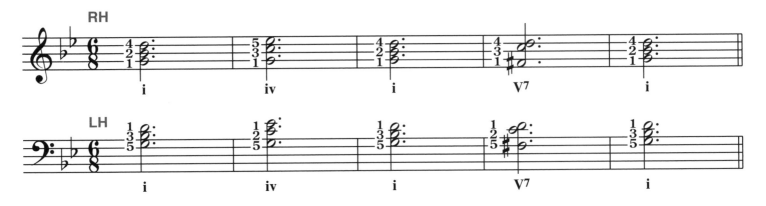

WHEN JOHNNY COMES MARCHING HOME

American Folk Song

*A whole rest means *rest for a whole measure in ANY time signature.*

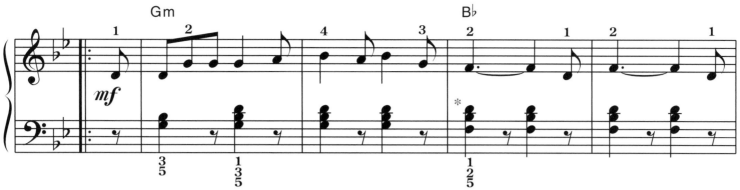

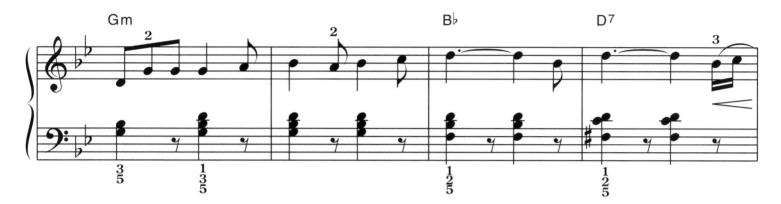

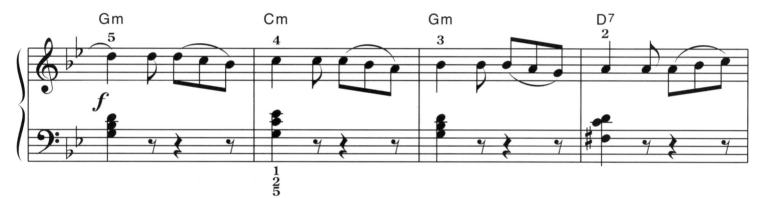

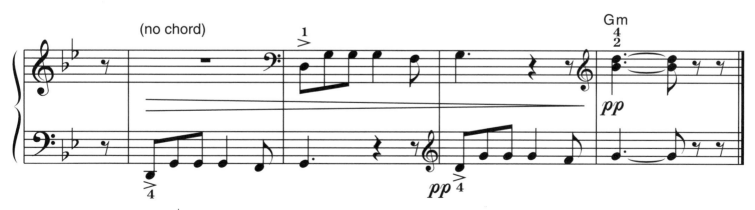

*This inversion of the B♭ MAJOR CHORD was used in the key of F MAJOR.

72

Reviewing: Major & Minor Triads

MAJOR TRIADS consist of a
ROOT, MAJOR 3rd, & PERFECT 5th.

MINOR TRIADS consist of a
ROOT, MINOR 3rd, & PERFECT 5th.

C MAJOR TRIAD =
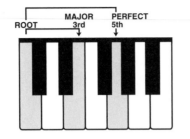

C MINOR TRIAD =
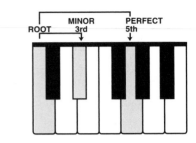

Any **MAJOR** triad may be changed to a **MINOR** triad by **LOWERING** the 3rd **ONE HALF STEP!**
Play a MAJOR triad, then a MINOR triad, on each note of the C MAJOR SCALE. Begin as shown
below. Play with LH, using 5 3 1 on each triad. Repeat *8va* with RH, using 1 3 5.

Introducing: Diminished Triads

The word DIMINISHED means "made smaller."
When a PERFECT 5th is made smaller by one half step, it becomes a DIMINISHED 5th.
A DIMINISHED TRIAD consists of a ROOT, MINOR 3rd, & DIMINISHED 5th.

C DIMINISHED TRIAD =
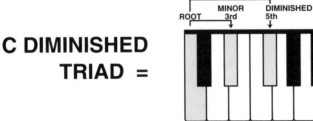

IMPORTANT!
It is helpful to note that
the interval between each
note of a DIMINISHED TRIAD
is **3 HALF STEPS!**

Any **MINOR** triad may be changed to a **DIMINISHED** triad by **LOWERING** the 5th **ONE HALF STEP!**
Play a MINOR triad, then a DIMINISHED triad, on each note of the C MAJOR SCALE. Begin as
shown below. Play with LH, using 5 3 1 on each triad. Repeat *8va* with RH, using 1 3 5.
The symbol for the diminished triad is **dim** (or ○).

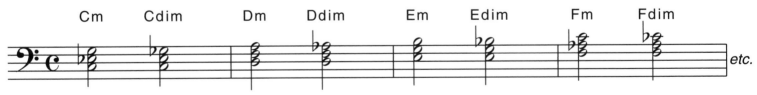

Any **MAJOR** triad may be changed to a **DIMINISHED** triad by **LOWERING** the 3rd & 5th **ONE HALF STEP!**
Play a MAJOR triad, then a DIMINISHED triad, on each note of the C MAJOR SCALE. Begin as shown
below. Play with LH, using 5 3 1 on each triad. Repeat *8va* with RH, using 1 3 5.

Theme from SYMPHONY NO. 6 (1st MOVEMENT)

This expressive theme from Peter Ilyich Tchaikovsky's 6th Symphony, known as
"The Pathetique Symphony," was the basis for a popular song.

Tchaikovsky

74

Play these measures several times to prepare for *FASCINATION.*

Fingering C chord with 4 2 1 makes
reaching down to G easier.

Play the 2nd (F & G) with
the side of the thumb!

FASCINATION

F. Marchetti

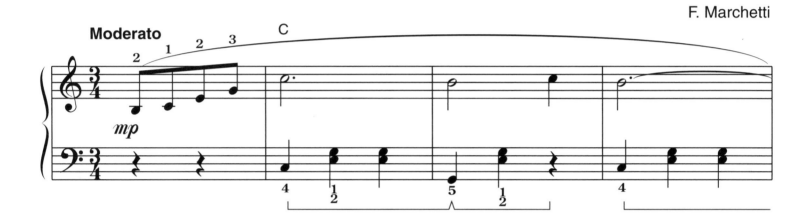

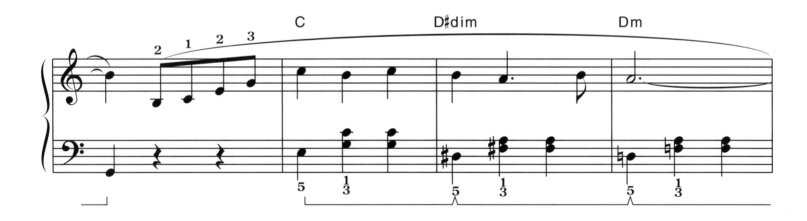

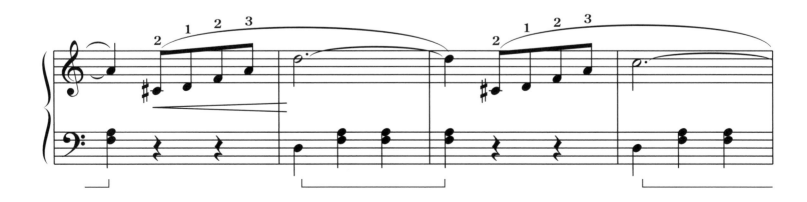

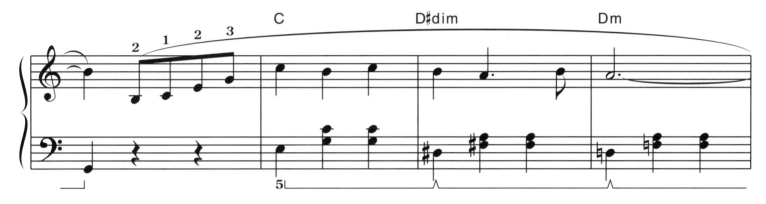

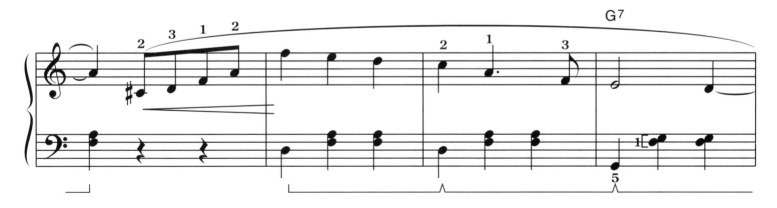

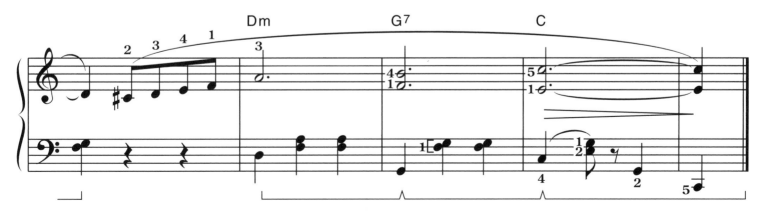

Introducing: Augmented Triads

The word AUGMENTED means "made larger." When a PERFECT 5th is made larger by one half step, it becomes an AUGMENTED 5th.

An AUGMENTED TRIAD consists of a ROOT, MAJOR 3rd, & AUGMENTED 5th.

AUGMENTED TRIAD =

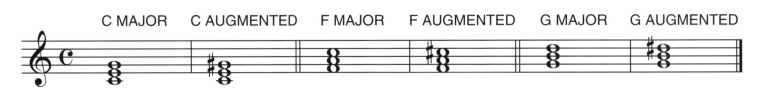

Any MAJOR triad may be changed to an AUGMENTED triad by raising the 5th ONE HALF STEP!

C MAJOR	C AUGMENTED	F MAJOR	F AUGMENTED	G MAJOR	G AUGMENTED

Play a MAJOR triad, then an AUGMENTED triad, on each note of the C MAJOR SCALE, as shown below. Play very slowly with LH, using 5 3 1 on each triad. Repeat *8va* with RH, using 1 3 5. The symbol for the augmented triad is **aug** (or **+**).

DOUBLE SHARP (✕)
Raises a sharped note another half step, or a natural note one whole step.

DEEP RIVER

Adagio moderato   Traditional

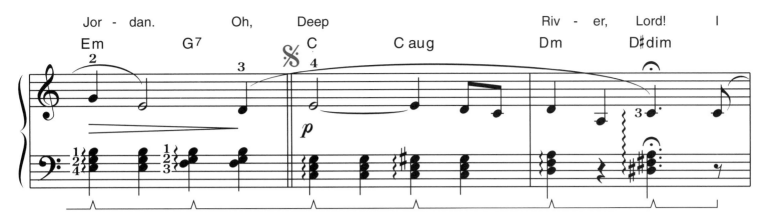

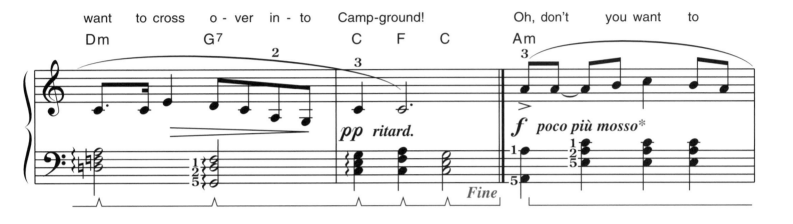

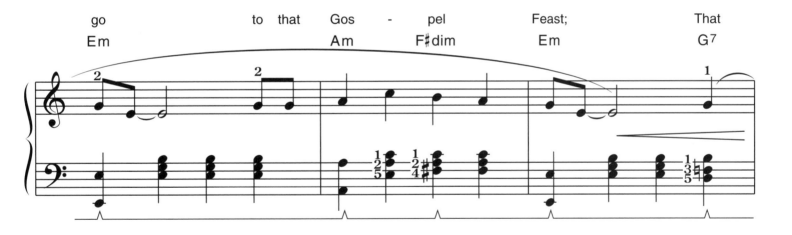

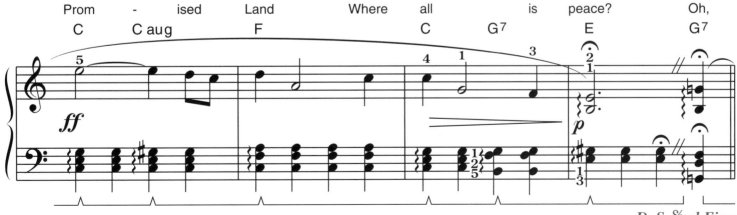

D. S. 𝄋 al Fine

(Repeat from the sign 𝄋, and play to the Fine.)

* *Poco più mosso* = a little faster.

The E♭ Major Scale

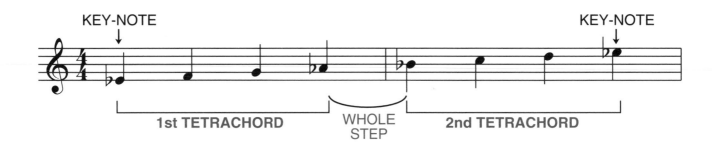

KEY-NOTE ↓   KEY-NOTE ↓

| 1st TETRACHORD | WHOLE STEP | 2nd TETRACHORD |

The 5th finger is not used in either hand in the E♭ MAJOR SCALE.
The key note, E♭, is played by the 3rd finger of the RH and the LH.

Play slowly and carefully!

KEY OF E♭ MAJOR
Key Signature: 3 flats (B♭, E♭, & A♭)

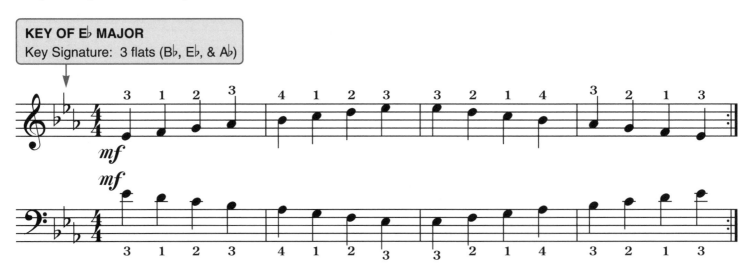

After you have learned to play the E♭ MAJOR SCALE with hands separate,
you may play the hands together in contrary motion. Both hands play the
same numbered fingers at the same time!

LOCH LOMOND

Traditional

Andante

By yon bon - nie banks and by yon bon - nie braes, Where the

mf espressivo

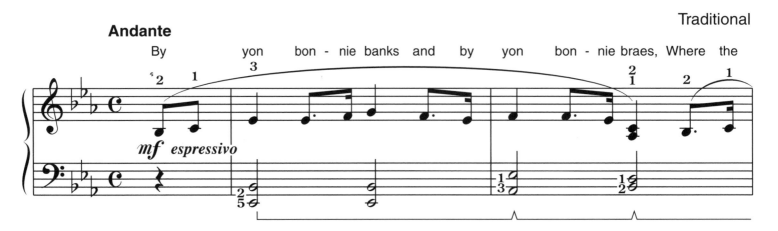

Risoluto*

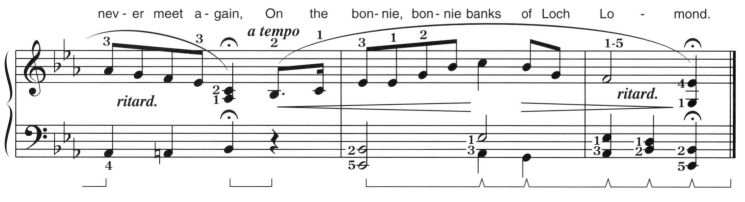

* **Risoluto** = resolutely.

The Primary Chords in E♭ Major

Reviewing the E♭ MAJOR SCALE, LH ascending.

KEY OF E♭ MAJOR
Key Signature: 3 flats (B♭, E♭ & A♭)

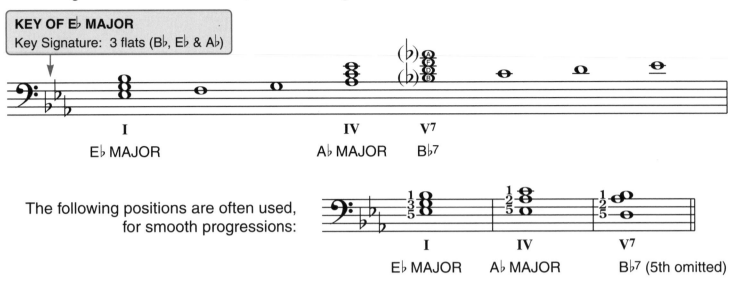

I	IV	V⁷
E♭ MAJOR	A♭ MAJOR	B♭⁷

The following positions are often used,
for smooth progressions:

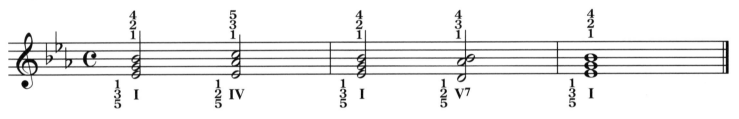

I	IV	V⁷
E♭ MAJOR	A♭ MAJOR	B♭⁷ (5th omitted)

E♭ MAJOR CHORD PROGRESSION with I, IV & V⁷ chords

Play with RH as written, then with LH one octave lower.

E♭ MAJOR PROGRESSION with broken I, IV & V⁷ chords. Play several times with LH.

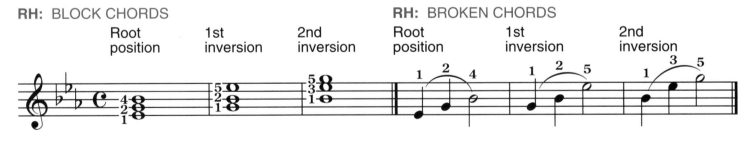

The next piece contains the E♭ MAJOR TRIAD in ALL POSITIONS.
Practice the following as a warm-up exercise.

RH: BLOCK CHORDS

Root position | 1st inversion | 2nd inversion

RH: BROKEN CHORDS

Root position | 1st inversion | 2nd inversion

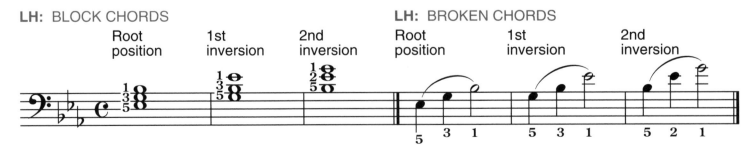

LH: BLOCK CHORDS

Root position | 1st inversion | 2nd inversion

LH: BROKEN CHORDS

Root position | 1st inversion | 2nd inversion

Aria from "THE MARRIAGE OF FIGARO"

This famous aria is prominently featured in the film, "Amadeus."

Andante maestoso

W. A. Mozart

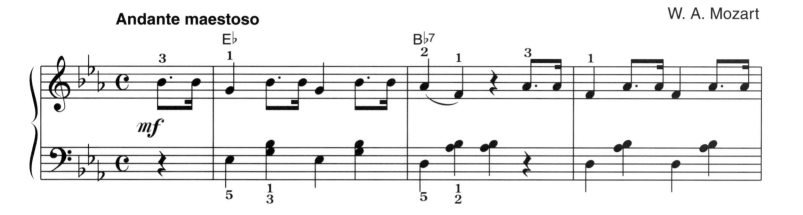

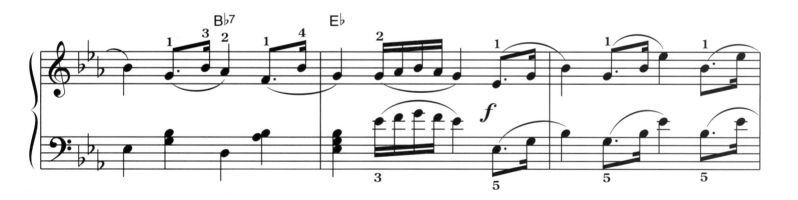

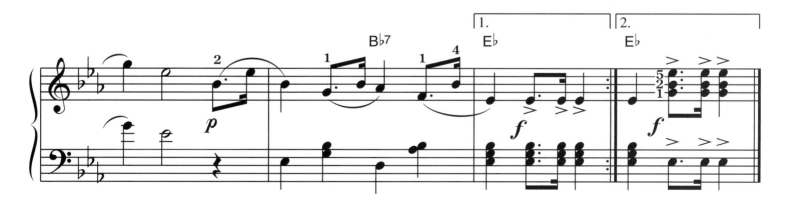

Introducing: The Trill

The TRILL is a rapid alternation of the written note with the note above it.
In some pieces, the trill is written out in notes. In others, a TRILL SIGN is used.

The most commonly used signs for the trill are: *tr* and *tr* 〰〰〰

In music of the 17th and 18th centuries, and most music of the early 19th century, the trill begins on the note ABOVE the written note. In later music the trill begins on the WRITTEN note. In *Alfred's Basic Adult Course,* you will always be shown how each trill should be played.

may be played: or

Trills do not always need to have an *exact* number of notes. They may be played faster than indicated above, with additional alternations of the two notes, but they must fit into the time value of the note.

MOZART'S TRILL EXERCISE

This valuable exercise was handed down to us by one of Mozart's most famous pupils, J. N. Hummel. If you practice it daily, you will be able to trill with all combinations of fingers with either hand!

Practice the entire exercise slowly at first. Gradually increase speed.

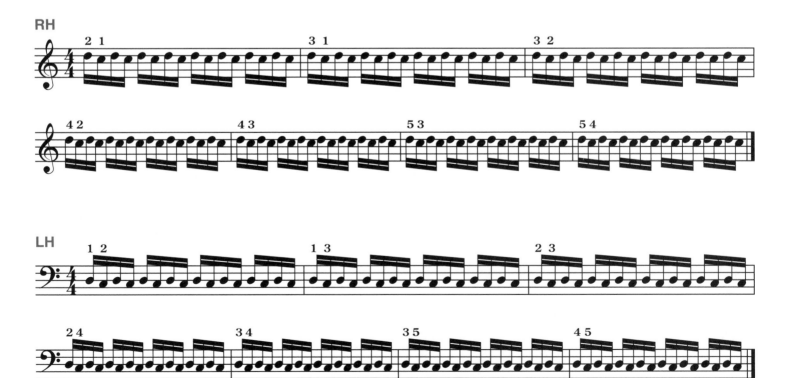

This piece is part of a larger composition for wind instruments, strings
and drums. It is typical of the festive music played in the French courts
in the early 1700s. It has become a familiar favorite because of its use
as the theme for the popular television series, *Masterpiece Theatre.*

Theme from a
FESTIVE RONDEAU

Jean Joseph Mouret (1682–1753)
Transcribed by P. M. L.

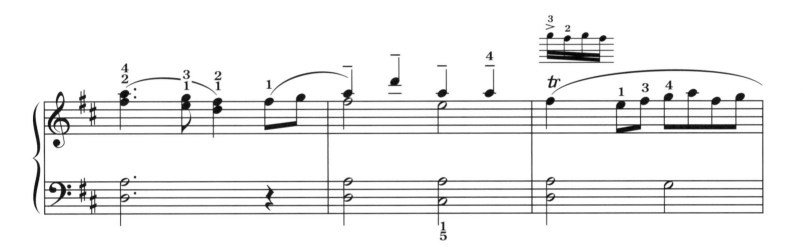

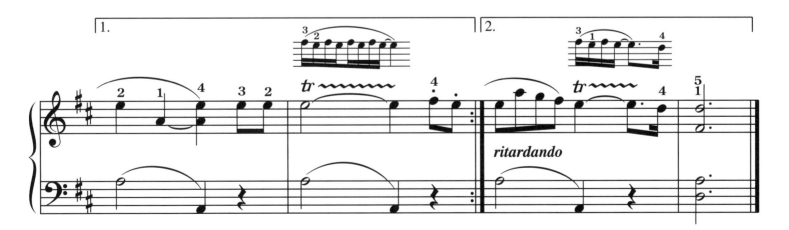

*The short line over or under the note or chord is a *tenuto* mark. *Tenuto* is an Italian word meaning "held."
  Play the note or chord with a slight stress and hold it for its *full value.*

PREPARATION FOR THE FOLLOWING PIECE

All the variations in the RH are based on this chord progression. Play it several times
before beginning the piece. Also play the LH of the piece several times.

Variations on the Theme
from the Celebrated
CANON IN D

Pachelbel's *CANON IN D* was used as background in
the film "Ordinary People," and has been heard in many
different settings, in supermarkets, movies, radio and
television productions. Everywhere!

Pachelbel

Andante moderato

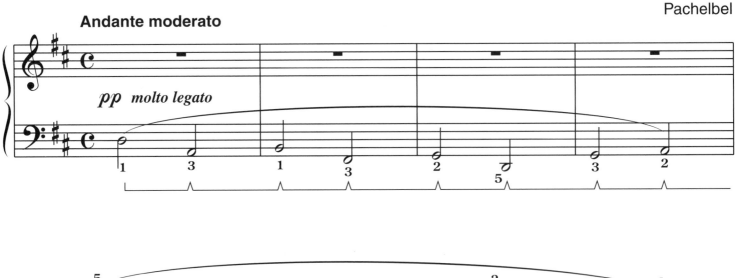

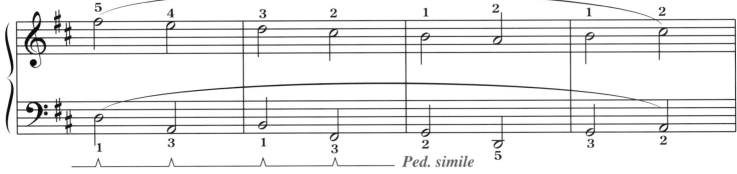

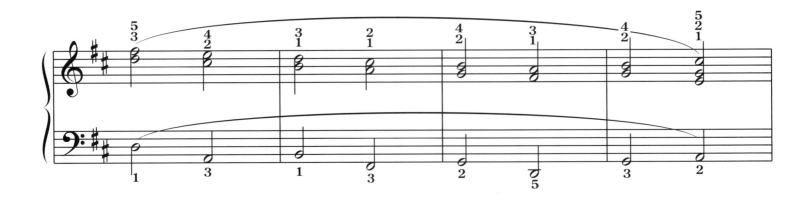

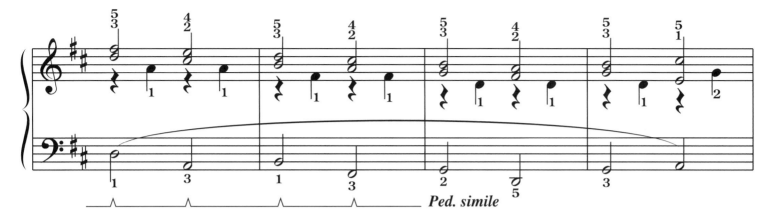

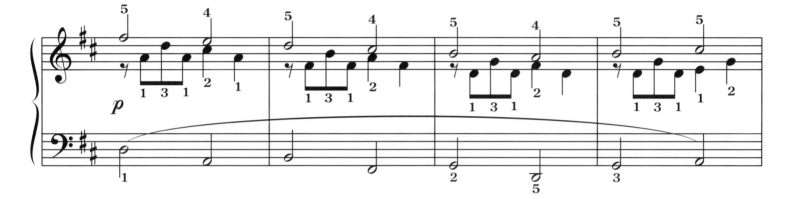

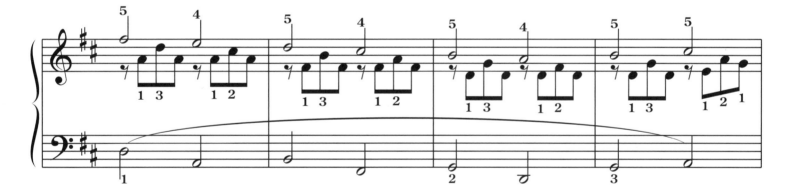

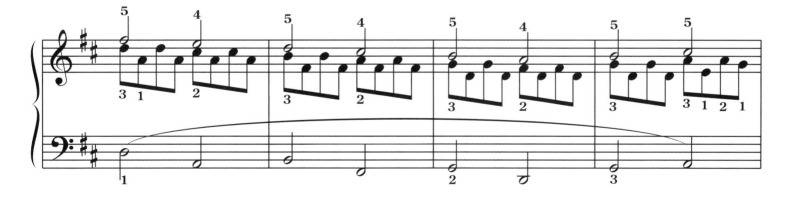

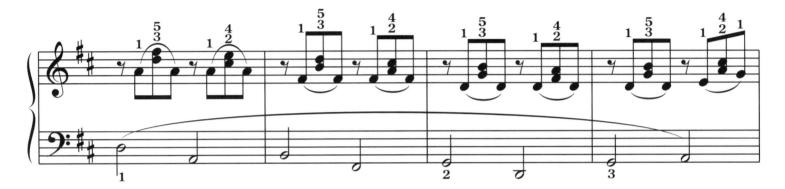

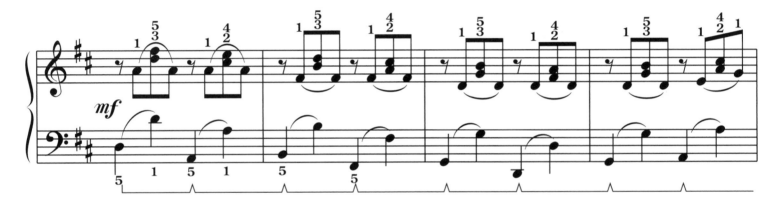

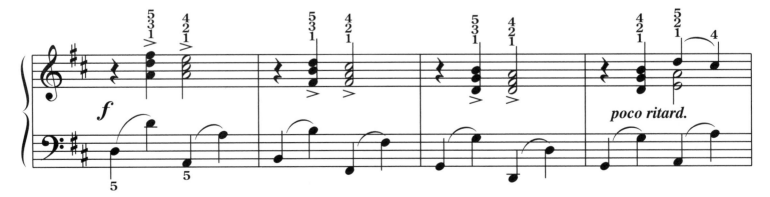

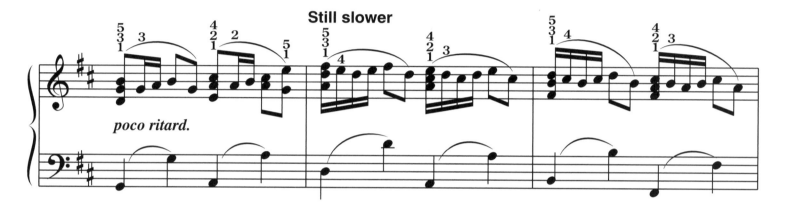

The Circle of 5ths—Major Keys

The CIRCLE OF FIFTHS is a useful tool for memorizing the order of keys, as well as the order in which the sharps or flats occur within the key signatures.

The circle is easy to memorize. Begin with the key of G, which contains 1 sharp, F♯, which is the first sharp that occurs in any key signature containing sharps. Moving CLOCKWISE, each new key has one more sharp than the key before. The order of the sharps in the key signatures can be learned by saying "Fat Cats Go Down Alleys, Eating Bread." Moving COUNTERCLOCKWISE, the first flat occurring in any key signature containing flats is B♭. The order in which flats occur is easily learned by spelling "B E A D" and then "G C F."

There are TWELVE different MAJOR keys, but three of them have 2 different names. Notice the bottom 3 keys of the circle. D♭ major may also be called C♯ major. G♭ may be called F♯, and C♭ may be called B. Keys that have 2 names are called ENHARMONIC KEYS.

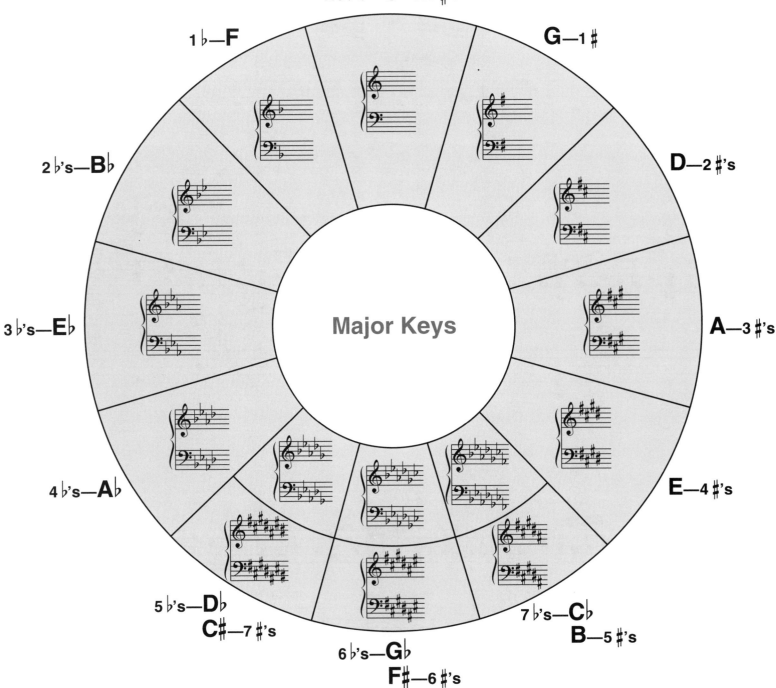

The Circle of 5ths—Minor Keys

There are also TWELVE different MINOR keys, three of which have 2 different names. The names of the keys around the circle are in the same order as those for the MAJOR keys, except we find **"a"** located at the top of the circle. (Lower case letters are used to indicate the names of the minor keys.) Each MINOR key is the relative of the MAJOR key found in the same position around the circle on the previous page.

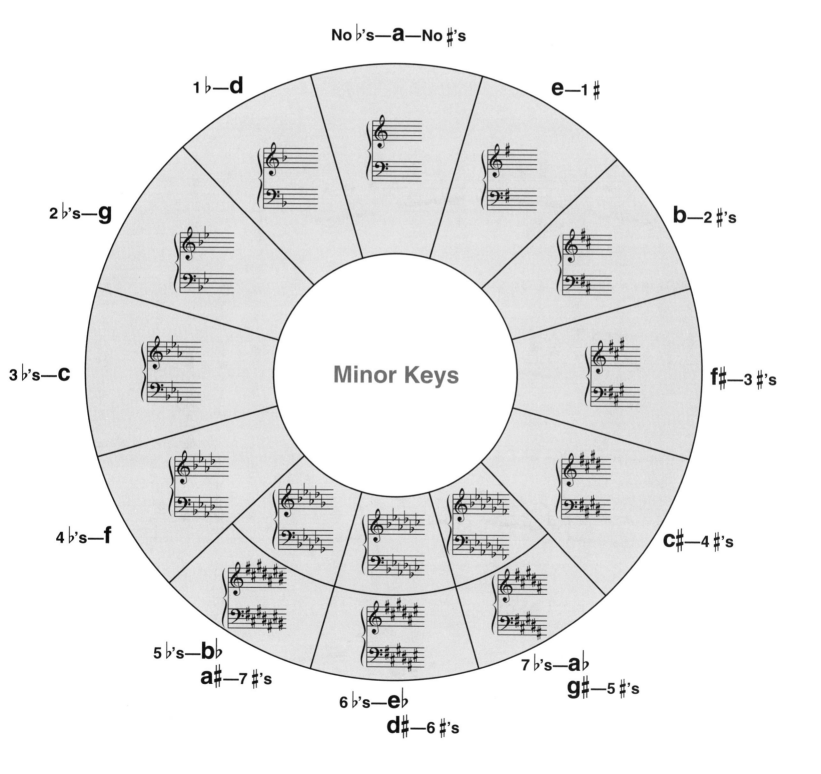

Major Scales and Primary Chords

C Major & Sharp Keys

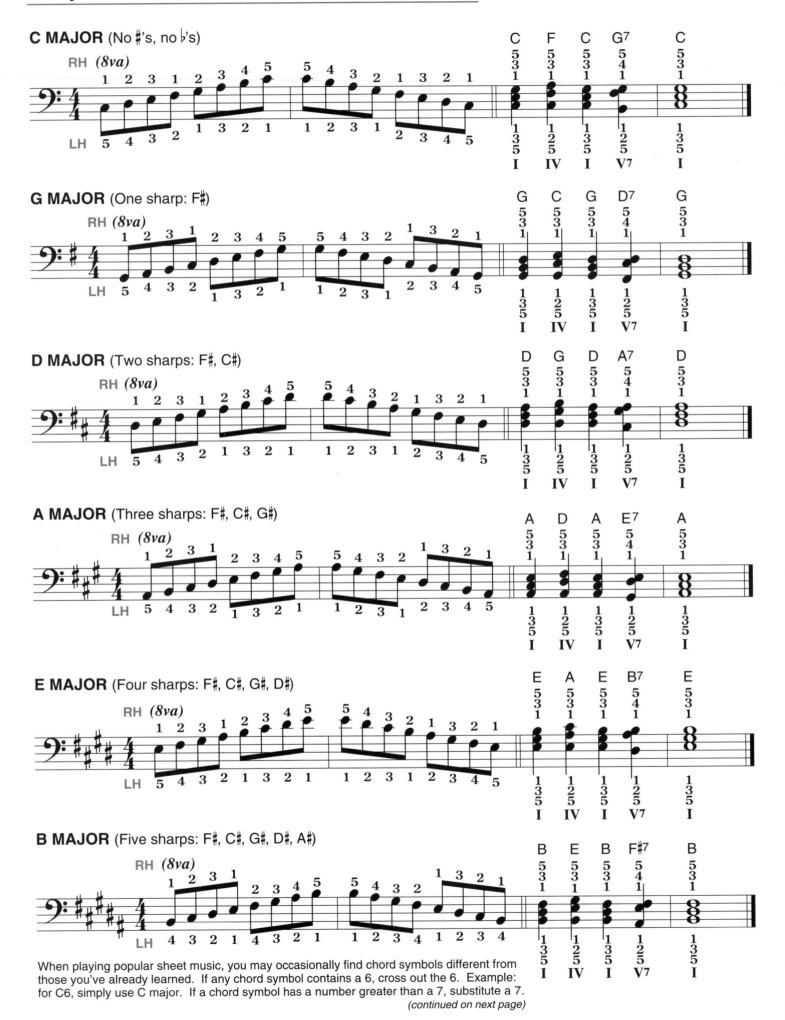

When playing popular sheet music, you may occasionally find chord symbols different from those you've already learned. If any chord symbol contains a 6, cross out the 6. Example: for C6, simply use C major. If a chord symbol has a number greater than a 7, substitute a 7.

(continued on next page)

Major Scales and Primary Chords

Flat Keys

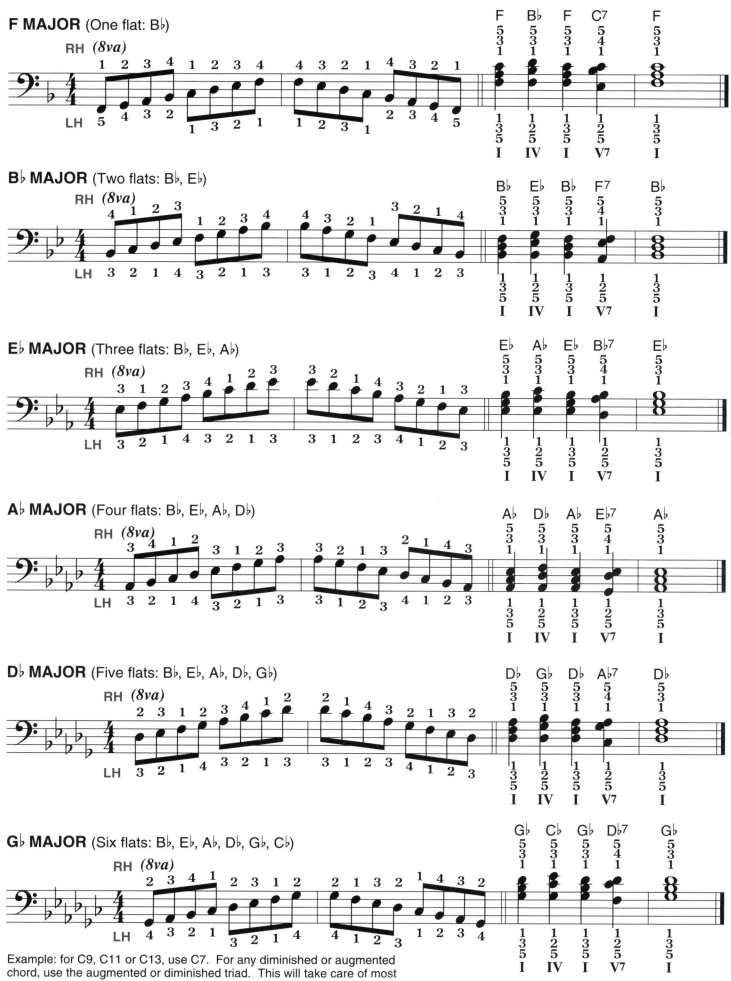

Example: for C9, C11 or C13, use C7. For any diminished or augmented chord, use the augmented or diminished triad. This will take care of most of the situations you are likely to encounter.

Harmonic Minor Scales and Primary Chords   A Minor & Sharp Keys

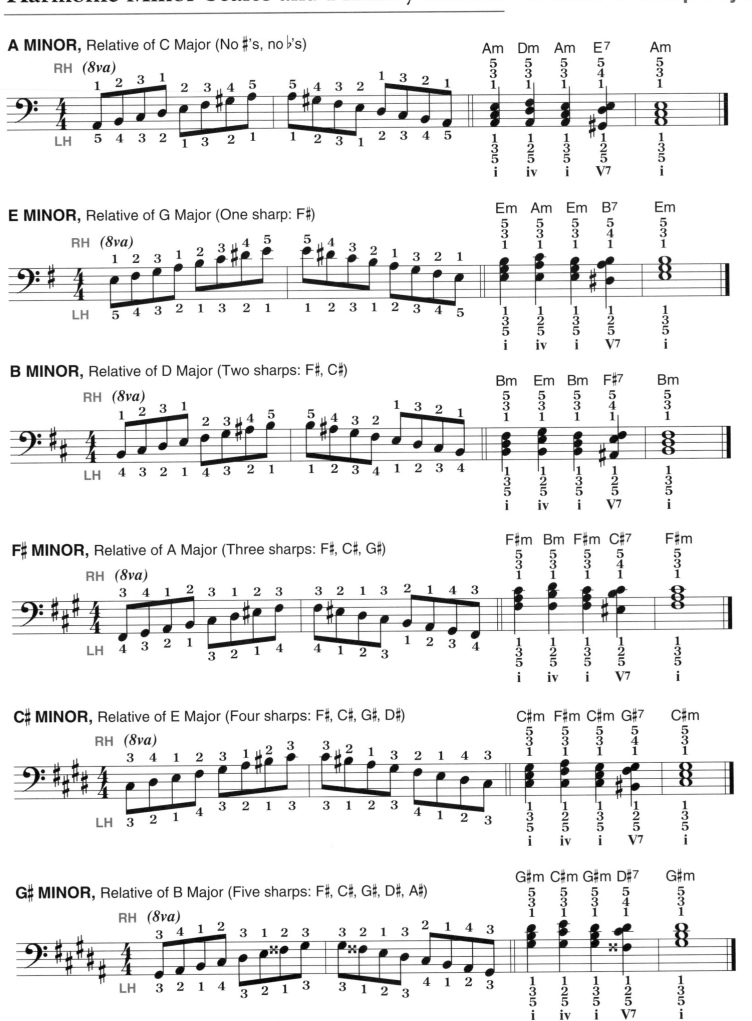

A MINOR, Relative of C Major (No #'s, no ♭'s)

E MINOR, Relative of G Major (One sharp: F#)

B MINOR, Relative of D Major (Two sharps: F#, C#)

F# MINOR, Relative of A Major (Three sharps: F#, C#, G#)

C# MINOR, Relative of E Major (Four sharps: F#, C#, G#, D#)

G# MINOR, Relative of B Major (Five sharps: F#, C#, G#, D#, A#)

Harmonic Minor Scales and Primary Chords   **Flat Keys**

Use these charts to form chords in any key!

Chord Chart

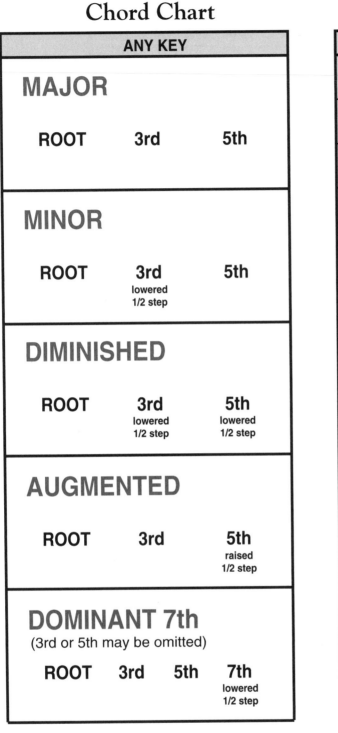

ANY KEY
MAJOR
ROOT 3rd 5th
MINOR
ROOT 3rd 5th lowered 1/2 step
DIMINISHED
ROOT 3rd 5th lowered 1/2 step lowered 1/2 step
AUGMENTED
ROOT 3rd 5th raised 1/2 step
DOMINANT 7th (3rd or 5th may be omitted) ROOT 3rd 5th 7th lowered 1/2 step

Major Scale Chart

ROOT	2nd	3rd	4th	5th	6th	7th	8th
A♭	B♭	C	D♭	E♭	F	G	A♭
A	B	C♯	D	E	F♯	G♯	A
B♭	C	D	E♭	F	G	A	B♭
B	C♯	D♯	E	F♯	G♯	A♯	B
C♭	D♭	E♭	F♭	G♭	A♭	B♭	C♭
C	D	E	F	G	A	B	C
C♯	D♯	E♯	F♯	G♯	A♯	B♯	C♯
D♭	E♭	F	G♭	A♭	B♭	C	D♭
D	E	F♯	G	A	B	C♯	D
E♭	F	G	A♭	B♭	C	D	E♭
E	F♯	G♯	A	B	C♯	D♯	E
F	G	A	B♭	C	D	E	F
F♯	G♯	A♯	B	C♯	D♯	E♯	F♯
G♭	A♭	B♭	C♭	D♭	E♭	F	G♭
G	A	B	C	D	E	F♯	G

HOW TO USE THE CHARTS

All chords are formed by combining certain tones of the major scale according to definite rules. For example, any MAJOR CHORD is formed by combining the ROOT, 3rd & 5th tones of the MAJOR SCALE of the same name. The chord may, of course, be inverted by moving the root to the top (3rd, 5th, ROOT) and again by moving the 3rd to the top (5th, ROOT, 3rd).

The construction of some chords involves lowering or raising one or more tones 1/2 step. For example, to form the C DIMINISHED CHORD, look up DIMINISHED in the chord chart on the left, above. Note that the diminished chord consists of ROOT, a 3rd lowered 1/2 step, and a 5th lowered 1/2 step. Look up the C MAJOR SCALE in the chart on the right, above. Note that the ROOT is C, the 3rd is E, and the 5th is G. Since the 3rd and 5th must be lowered, make each of these FLAT (play the next key to the left, black or white); thus the C DIMINISHED CHORD is C E♭ G♭. The chord may be inverted, of course.

Dictionary of Musical Terms

Accelerando . . . . . gradually increasing in speed

Accent sign (>) . . play with special emphasis

Adagio . . . . slow

Allargando . . . . . . becoming slower and broader

Allegro . . . . quickly, happily, fast

Andante . . . . moving along (walking speed)

A tempo . . . . resume original speed

Cantabile . . . . in a singing style

Coda . . . . an added ending

Coda sign (⊕) . . . . indication to proceed to CODA

Common time (𝄴) . same as 4/4 time

Contrary motion . . hands moving in opposite directions

Crescendo (⟨) . gradually louder

Da Capo al Fine . . repeat from the beginning to the word "Fine"

Decrescendo . . . . gradually softer (same as "diminuendo")

Dal Segno al Fine . repeat from the sign 𝄋 to the word "Fine"

Diminuendo (⟩) gradually softer

Dolce . . . . sweetly

Double flat (𝄫) . . . lowers a flatted note 1/2 step, or a natural note one whole step

Double sharp (𝄪) . . raises a sharped note 1/2 step, or a natural note one whole step

Espressivo . . . . . . expressively

Fermata (⌢) . . . . . hold the note or notes under the sign longer

Fine . . . . the end

Forte (𝆑) . . . . loud

Fortissimo (𝆑𝆑) . . . very loud

Grazioso . . . . gracefully

Interval . . . . the distance from one note to the next

Largo . . . . very slow

Legato . . . . smoothly connected

Loco . . . . as written (not *8va*)

Maestoso . . . . majestically

Mezzo forte . . . . . . moderately loud

Mezzo piano . . . . . moderately soft

Moderato . . . . a moderate speed

Molto . . . . much, very

Morendo . . . . dying away

Octave sign (*8va*) . play 8 scale tones (one octave) higher when the sign is above the notes; 8 scale tones lower when the sign is below the notes.

Pianissimo (*pp*) . . very soft

Piano (*p*) . . . . soft

Più mosso . . . . faster

Poco . . . . little, small

Poco a poco . . . . . little by little

Prestissimo . . . . . very fast

Presto . . . . fast

Repeat sign (𝄇) repeat from the beginning, or from 𝄆

Risoluto . . . . resolutely

Ritardando . . . . . . slowing

Scherzo . . . . a musical joke

Segue . . . . continue

Sforzando . . . . forcing; suddenly loud on one note or chord

Simile . . . . continue in the same manner

Staccato . . . . short, detached notes

Tempo . . . . rate of speed

Tenuto (–) . . . . hold for full value; emphasize slightly

Tetrachord . . . . . . 4 tones having a pattern of whole step–whole step–half step

Certificate of Award

This is to certify that

_____

has sucessfully completed

Alfred's Basic Adult Piano Course, Level 2

and is hereby promoted to

Alfred's Basic Adult Course, Lesson Book 3.

_____
Date

_____
Teacher